BEYOND THE IDEA

Also by Vijay Govindarajan and Chris Trimble

How Stella Saved the Farm
The Other Side of Innovation
Reverse Innovation
Ten Rules for Strategic Innovators

BEYOND
THE
IDEA

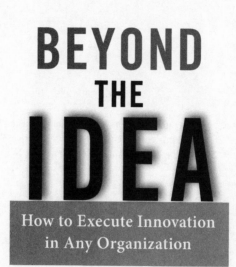

How to Execute Innovation
in Any Organization

VIJAY GOVINDARAJAN and **CHRIS TRIMBLE**

St. Martin's Press 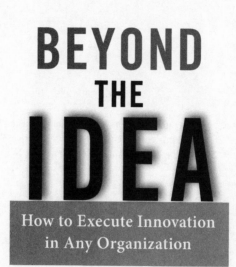 New York

www.stmartins.com

Design by Maura Rosenthal / Mspace

Library of Congress Cataloging-in-Publication Data

Govindarajan, Vijay.
    Beyond the idea : how to execute innovation in any organization /
Vijay Govindarajan, Chris Trimble.
        pp. cm.
    ISBN 978-1-250-04017-6 (hardcover)
    ISBN 978-1-4668-3541-2 (e-book)
    1. Diffusion of innovations—Management.   2. Technological
innovations—Management.   3. New products.   4. Creative ability
in business.   I. Trimble, Chris.   II. Title.
    HD45.G6185 2013
    658.5'14—dc23

                                                        2013013487

St. Martin's Press books may be purchased for educational, business, or promotional use. For information on bulk purchases, please contact Macmillan Corporate and Premium Sales Department at 1-800-221-7945, extension 5442, or write specialmarkets@macmillan.com.

First Edition: September 2013

10   9   8   7   6   5   4   3   2   1

CONTENTS

Part II—Model C: Build the Team

Part III—Model C: Create the Plan

CONTENTS

PREFACE

Thomas Edison said it over a century ago: *Genius is 1 percent inspiration, 99 percent perspiration.*

Unfortunately, no one listened. When companies launch innovation initiatives, they typically allot almost all of their time and energy to that initial 1 percent—the thrilling hunt for the breakthrough idea. The real innovation challenge, however, lies beyond the idea. It lies in a long, hard journey—from imagination to impact.

Even the best-managed corporations in the world struggle to execute innovation initiatives. This challenge, which we call the *other side* of innovation, is widely misunderstood. Some companies conflate this side and the other side, believing it is all the same. Others imagine that executing an innovation initiative can't be much different than executing day-to-day operations. Both views are wrong. Innovation execution is neither innovation nor execution. It is its own unique beast.

Since the fall of 2000, we have been deeply immersed in studying just this one topic. Along the way, we have produced three books. *The Other Side of Innovation: Solving the Execution Challenge* (2010) was a general treatment of all innovation initiatives; *Reverse Innovation: Create Far from Home, Win Everywhere* (2012) examined the specific challenge of innovating to serve customers in the rapidly growing emerging economies; and *Ten Rules for Strategic Innovators: From Idea to Execution* (2005) focused on high-risk but high-growth potential new ventures inside established organizations.

Along the way, we have both spent an enormous amount of time on the road, giving speeches, making presentations, and delivering workshops to as wide a range of industries as possible. We very often hear things like: "I couldn't agree with what you are saying any more thoroughly. But I really need you to spread the word to my colleagues." (If we only had a nickel for each time we've heard this request!)

There is, of course, a limit to how many people we can reach by boarding airplanes and making presentations. There are just the two of us. And yet, we've seen that in order for a company to achieve innovation success, a *lot* of people have to understand what to do. One person is not enough; ten working on the same innovation challenge is closer to the mark.

Traditional business books, however, have limitations that prevent them from reaching high concentrations of people in a single organization. *Why?* Number one on the list: People are extremely busy. We are very proud of the clarity and readability of our prior books, but we understand that each takes several hours and several sittings to read. Many executives simply don't have that kind of time.

Therefore, this year, we published two books. Our favorite attribute of both of these books is that they are *short*.

Earlier in 2013, we published *How Stella Saved the Farm: A Tale About Making Innovation Happen*. It is a simple parable about a farm in trouble and how the farm innovates to get out of trouble. Though we don't pretend to have matched his literary achievement, we wrote *Stella* in the spirit of George Orwell's *Animal Farm*. It is a story about animals who run their own farm; it is also a light read with a very serious intent. Though *Stella* takes only about an hour to read, it still delivers the most fundamental principles at the core of *The Other Side of Innovation*. (To multiply *Stella*'s impact, we have developed related tools, discussion guides, and workshops, in partnership with the International Thought Leader Network. Please visit *Stella*'s website: howstellasavedthefarm.com.)

In *Beyond the Idea,* our intent is to convey "Here's what you should do" and "Here's why it works" in the most direct, clear, and compact way possible. We've provided readers a much greater level of specificity than was possible in *Stella,* but we've nonetheless kept this book concise.

This book includes several critical expansions beyond *The Other Side of Innovation*. Chapters 2, 3, 5, and 9 include new ideas that we now know are critical for gaining buy-in and understanding. That said, readers of our past books may feel that they've read much of what's in these pages before. This is a reasonable reaction. We hope that *Beyond the Idea*'s primary impact is not in its intellectual advance, but in its accessibility. Indeed, we hope that the book's brevity will help push the management profession one step closer to a state of sophistication wherein practices for managing all forms of innovation are as well understood and systematically practiced as those for quality improvement; as frequently talked about as TQM and Six Sigma.

To slim *Beyond the Idea* down to its very compact format, we've had to make some choices. Most critically, we've chosen to eliminate the detailed examples that are the hallmarks of our past works. We know that rich examples make concepts more concrete for many readers. We ask such readers to consider reading *Beyond the Idea* in conjunction with *Stella,* which is actually a composite of dozens of case studies we've written over the years. Indeed, every detail in *Stella,* save those obviously intended to amuse, are drawn from real observations at real companies. Alternatively, there are many examples in our past books and articles, and all of our case studies are freely available on the website for *The Other Side of Innovation,* theothersideofinnovation.com. We do use a select handful of brief company examples in *Beyond the Idea*. All are drawn either from these case studies or from interviews with company executives. There is one exception, Toyota. Here, we drew heavily from Steven J. Spear and H. Kent Bowen's *Harvard Business Review* article, "Decoding the DNA of the Toyota Production System" (September 1999).

We have chosen not to provide footnotes in *Beyond the Idea*. We ask readers interested in examining the formal academic underpinnings of our work to refer to our prior books.

While we believe that we must reach a greater concentration of readers per company to have the impact that we desire, we don't imagine that every employee needs to understand every word in *Beyond the Idea*. For your own company, it may be useful to think about achieving four levels of understanding, depending on position, as outlined in the table below:

Level	Chapters	Who?
1	1	All employees.
2	1–4	All managers.
3	1–4, 5, 9	All in the vicinity of Model C initiatives. (These are the higher degree of difficulty initiatives, as we will define shortly.)
4	All	Those directly involved in Model C initiatives.

Please reach us by e-mail (vg@dartmouth.edu, chris .trimble@dartmouth.edu) to share your thoughts.

Best wishes,

Vijay Govindarajan

Chris Trimble

September 2013

Dartmouth College

Hanover, New Hampshire

THREE MODELS FOR MAKING INNOVATION HAPPEN

CHAPTER 1

THE OTHER SIDE OF INNOVATION

nnovation is a two-part challenge. Part one is ideas; part two is execution.

To win, you have to succeed at both. Many companies, however, expend most or nearly all of their energies on part one. As such, they tend to produce a great many ideas on paper that never become anything more than . . . ideas on paper.

The most important message in *Beyond the Idea* is very simple: Part two, innovation execution, is its own unique discipline. It requires time, energy, and distinct thinking. Unfortunately, few companies treat it as such. In fact, few companies give it much thought at all.

FIRST, SHIFT ATTENTION TO EXECUTION

Companies wishing to improve at innovation must shift a substantial portion of their time and energy to part two, the other side of innovation. Doing so is not easy. The gravitational pull toward the front end of innovation is powerful. For one thing, the front end has the natural advantage of being first in the sequence. You can't even get started without an idea!

That's not all. Most everyone instinctively agrees that the world needs more front-end activity—more imagination, more creativity, more out-of-the-box thinking. Strategists see innovation as the pathway to disrupting your competition. Scientists and engineers link innovation to technological breakthroughs. Romantics see innovation as dramatic advances delivered by chance meetings and chance occurrences; by magic and by luck.

And then there is the icing on the cake—the rewards. We put idea people on a pedestal. We celebrate them, we promote them. We mythologize inventors and their inventions.

As such, it's a snap to entice people into the front end. Getting people to attend creative brainstorming sessions, for example, rarely requires heavy persuasion. The front end offers the possibility of an exciting discovery, a eureka moment, an unexpected insight. It is, plainly put, fun.

The other side of innovation, on the other hand, is about practical matters. It is about getting the work done. It is blood, sweat, and tears. It is, plainly put, less fun.

Indeed, many people withdraw when it comes time to execute. Suddenly, innovation becomes just one more thing on a crowded agenda. Rather than the promise of outsize rewards, many will anticipate being blamed if the initiative does not go as well as hoped.

No wonder, then, that the front end gets all of the attention. No wonder that part two lives in part one's long shadow. This imbalance of attention shows up on many maps that companies create of the innovation process. The typical map breaks down the front end of innovation into several substeps—for example, generating ideas, cross-pollinating ideas, evaluating ideas, selecting the best ideas. Then, on the far right side of the page, just barely hanging on in the consciousness of the mapmakers, is that one final step: execution.

These maps speak volumes. They show just how dramatically innovation execution is underestimated. The attitude is: The real innovation challenge is the epic search for the breakthrough idea! What is part two? That's just getting the work done!

Be careful. Many companies are quite confident that they excel at execution of day-to-day operations. Therefore, they mistakenly conclude, they must be equally good at executing innovation. Unfortunately, comparing the two is like comparing a simple somersault to a triple flip with a quadruple twist. There really is no comparison.

ORGANIZATIONS ARE NOT BUILT TO EXECUTE INNOVATION

So why is innovation execution so hard? Simply put, organizations are not built for it. Quite to the contrary, they are built for ongoing operations. They are built to be *Performance Engines*.

A well-run Performance Engine is the master of many challenges. It excels at serving today's customers and fighting today's rivals. It is terrific at driving for efficiency by holding employees accountable. It is on time, on budget, and on spec—every day, every week, and every month. It delivers bottom-line results each and every quarter. Like a finely crafted Swiss timepiece, a great Performance Engine never misses a beat.

As impressive as this may be, the Performance Engine confronts innovation with high hurdles. Innovation promises short-term pain for long-term gain, but the Performance Engine wants to win *now*. Innovation requires experimentation; the Performance Engine demands efficiency. Innovations sometimes fail; the Performance Engine struggles to forgive.

These contrasts illustrate the first law of the other side of innovation: *Innovation and ongoing operations are always and inevitably in conflict.*

One indicator of just how deep the incompatibilities run is the fundamental accounting premise that a business is an *ongoing concern,* meaning that the current period will look an awful lot like the prior one. This is, of course, the antithesis of innovation.

The most fundamental source of conflict, however, lies in the *method* of the Performance Engine. This method is the same in every industry, in every part of the world, and in every type of organization—including private sector, public sector, and social sector organizations. It is to try to make every process and every activity as *repeatable* and as *predictable* as possible.

There is great power in both. When a process is repeatable, it is possible to break the process into small tasks and have people specialize. For centuries, specialization of labor has been recognized as a remarkable expedient to efficiency. Of equal importance, when a process becomes predictable, performance standards can be set and employees can be held accountable for very specific and quantified results.

Repeatability and predictability may be foundational for the Performance Engine, but they are also the antithesis of innovation. Far from being repeatable, innovation initiatives are intentional departures from the past. Far from being predictable, innovation initiatives proceed into territory in which there is no precedent upon which to base any forecast.

The Performance Engine strives for *repeatable* and *predictable,* but innovation is, by nature, *nonroutine* and *uncertain.* These are the *fundamental incompatibilities* between innovation and ongoing operations. They strike right at the heart of how managers are trained and how organizations are designed.

FUNDAMENTAL INCOMPATIBILITIES		
METHOD OF THE PERFORMANCE ENGINE	Repeatability	Predictability
REALITIES OF INNOVATION	Non-Routine	Uncertain

With such deep incompatibilities, perhaps the solution is to tear down the Performance Engine and rebuild organizations from scratch! Alas, we cannot. It is not that simple.

A well-run Performance Engine is a very powerful asset. Indeed, it is the foundation for an organization's well-being. Great companies have great Performance Engines. Without one, customers leave, costs rise, profits fall, and organizations fall apart.

There may be deep incompatibilities, but that does not make the Performance Engine the enemy. In fact, without profits from the Performance Engine, there is no funding for innovation. Furthermore, the aspiration of every innovation initiative is to someday be just like the Performance Engine—successful, stable, and profitable.

Therefore, throughout this book, we have taken as our first obligation that we must *do no harm*. The challenge is not just to make innovation happen, but to do so while simultaneously excelling at ongoing operations. The challenge is to tackle two very different activities—in fact, two diametrically opposed activities—at the same time.

We think you will agree, then, that we have our work cut out for us.

LET'S DEFINE TERMS

Learning about innovation can feel daunting, in part because there are so many innovation types. Beyond the familiar distinction between sustaining and disruptive categories, innovations have also been described as incremental, radical, strategic, reverse, architectural, modular, competence enhancing, and competence destroying. There are also process innovations, product innovations, adjacency innovations, and business model innovations. It is enough to make your head spin.

These categorizations are useful—but only on the front end of innovation. When setting strategy, when selecting the best of many possible ideas, or when trying to estimate an innovation's potential market impact, understanding the distinctions between the many innovation types can help.

The good news for *Beyond the Idea,* however, is that all of these categorizations are absolutely irrelevant on the other side. As such, we can leave this complexity behind and go with a very simple definition: An *innovation initiative* is any *project* that is *new* to your organization (not necessarily new to the world) and has an *uncertain* outcome.

Definition of an Innovation Initiative

Any *project* that is *new to your organization* and has an *uncertain outcome.*

The word *project* is important. On the other side of innovation, *ideas* become *projects* that need to be executed. In a sense, *Beyond the Idea* is about project management. That makes it sound pedestrian, but our focus is on projects that carry a high degree of difficulty because they are new and uncertain, and because they are in direct conflict with the Performance Engine. This takes us well outside of the realm of traditional project management techniques—which presume that a project has a precedent, that the necessary resources are well understood and available, and that the outcomes are relatively predictable.

Many people may want to judge some initiatives as more "innovative" than others. Some may even want to draw a line. *These* initiatives "count" as innovative, *those* do not. However, we have never found it to be useful to try to assess "innovativeness" or to draw a line that excludes some initiatives. The criteria for doing so are inevitably vague. Besides, doing so only seems to start arguments and diminish those whose ideas are deemed "less innovative" or "not innovative."

Therefore, for our purposes, any initiative that is new to your organization and has an uncertain outcome "counts" as innovation. Our definition is deliberately broad and inclusive.

That said, not all innovation initiatives are equally difficult to execute. We will find it quite useful to imagine a spectrum, from those that are relatively easy to those that are extremely difficult. (We are rating the

INNOVATION SPECTRUM

Easier ⟵——————⟶ Harder

Anything One Person Can
Tackle on Their Own Initiative
and in Their Free Time

A High-Risk
High-Growth Potential
New Venture

managerial degree of difficulty, which might be quite different from the *technological* degree of difficulty.) At the far left end of the spectrum are projects that any one employee might execute on their own initiative and in their free time—something as simple, for example, as a salesperson trying a new sales pitch. On the far right end of the spectrum lie high-risk, high-growth-potential new ventures.

ONLY THREE MODELS MAKE SENSE

Our research has shown us that there are *three distinct models for executing innovation initiatives*. We will call them Model S, Model R, and Model C—for Small, Repeatable, and Custom initiatives.

Three Models for
Executing Innovation Initiatives

Model	Type of Initiative
S	Small
R	Repeatable
C	Custom

All three models are important. All three models are powerful. Furthermore, companies need not commit to just one of the three models. All three can be used simultaneously.

However, *each initiative must be matched with the proper model for execution.* There is only one correct answer per initiative. So, a single company can have multiple Model S initiatives, multiple Model R initiatives, and multiple Model C initiatives at any one moment. How-

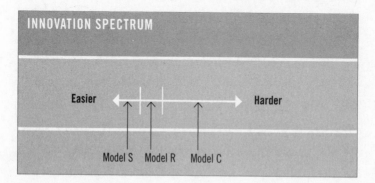

ever, trying to execute a Model C initiative with a Model R approach (or any other possible mismatch) is a recipe for heartaches and headaches.

To match each initiative to the right model, it is crucial to understand that Models S and R have brick-wall limitations. These models will only take you so far across the innovation spectrum, which is why Model C is so crucial. It is the most robust of the three, but also the most difficult and the least familiar.

The principles, mechanics, and limitations of the three models will become clear over the next three chapters. In the remainder of this chapter, we introduce just the basics.

WORKING AROUND THE PERFORMANCE ENGINE

The fundamental incompatibilities between innovation and ongoing operations are daunting, but there is more than one way to deal with them. Each of the three models, in fact, has a distinct strategy.

Model S recognizes that even the most efficient and tightly managed Performance Engines fall short of perfection. There is always at least some slack in the system, and that slack can be put to work for innovation. Model S's core strategy is to try to squeeze innovation into the slack. This is certainly possible, at least for small initiatives.

The philosophy underlying Model R is completely

different. It is to try to make innovation as repeatable and predictable as possible, just like the Performance Engine. This can also work, but only when a company executes a *series* of *similar* innovation initiatives.

Initiatives that are too big for Model S or too different from past efforts for Model R require the third option, Model C. Here, the fundamental incompatibilities between innovation and ongoing operations are severe, and can only be addressed by *separating* some of the innovation work from that of ongoing operations.

The three models, their strategies for dealing with the Performance Engine, and the types of initiatives they can produce are summarized below.

Each Model Has Its Own
Strategy for Dealing with the
Performance Engine

Model	Strategy for Dealing with the Performance Engine	What It Delivers
S Small	**Squeeze It In** Squeeze innovation into the slack in the system	A very large number of very small initiatives
R Repeatable	**Make It Repeatable and Predictable** Make innovation look as much like day-to-day operations as possible	A series of similar initiatives
C Custom	**Separate It** Separate incompatible innovation tasks from day-to-day operations	One unique initiative at a time

WHERE DO THE
RESOURCES COME FROM?

Beyond a distinct strategy for dealing with the Performance Engine, each of the three models has its own approach to acquiring the resources needed to make innovation happen. Anyone who has worked for an established organization knows that resources for innovation are difficult to come by. Nearly all resources are consumed by the Performance Engine.

Dividing the resources that an organization expends into two categories—resources allocated to ongoing operations and resources allocated to innovation initiatives—proves useful:

$$R_{tot} = R_{ops} + R_{inn}$$

Generally speaking, this division of resources is not one that is explicitly considered or budgeted. Instead, it is the result of many decisions. Some are made in formal plans while others are made informally, such as the choices employees make each day about how to allocate their time.

As it turns out, *time* is a critically important innovation resource. After, all, most initiatives start small, with just one or a few employees and a fraction of their time. Nonetheless, the resource of time often remains hidden from formal innovation plans. In general, companies spend far too little time thinking about it.

A chart that is rectangular but otherwise similar to a pie chart is helpful in visualizing the resource of people's time. The people in an organization are on the horizontal axis, from 0 to 100 percent, and their time on the vertical axis, from 0 to 100 percent.

Of course, most of people's time is consumed by ongoing operations. If you were to ask a sampling of employees in your organization what fraction of their time is left over for innovation after their obligations to the Performance Engine have been met, what do you suspect the average response would be? Ten percent? Five percent? Two percent?

So, how can innovation be squeezed in? One possibility, certainly, is to ask everyone to be an innovator during their slack time, which appears as a thin horizontal stripe across the top of the chart. Alternatively, a small group of people could be asked to dedicate *all* of their time to innovation. This would show up as a small vertical stripe at the right side of the chart. Some combination of both is also possible.

Indeed, one of the keys to success on the other side of innovation is simply breaking innovation initiatives into tasks, and assigning tasks to people. This sounds simple. In fact, it sounds like basic project management blocking and tackling.

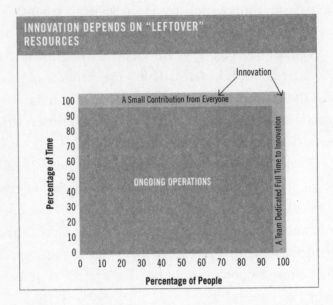

Nonetheless, well-managed companies get this wrong all of the time. There is a hidden dimension of trickiness for innovation initiatives: It makes a great deal of difference which tasks are assigned to people working on innovation full-time (the vertical stripe on the chart) and which are assigned to people working on innovation only part-time (the horizontal stripe on the chart)—and the distinction is vastly underappreciated.

In subsequent chapters, we will fill in the table below, showing how each of the three models takes a distinct approach to assigning innovation tasks to people, full-time and part-time.

Assigning Innovation Tasks to
Part-Time and Full-Time Innovators

Model	Part-Time	Full-Time
S Small		
R Repeatable		
C Custom		

CHAPTER 2

MODEL S
IS FOR SMALL INITIATIVES

M any organizations like to brag that they have a strong *culture of innovation*. In fact, the aspiration to create such a culture seems nearly universal. The desire is that every employee feels that they can be an innovator, every day. Everyone can come up with ideas. Everyone can even take some initiative to make things happen. Decades ago, Toyota famously created a culture of innovation, engaging front-line manufacturing employees in continuous improvement.

Of the three models, only Model S maps well to this popular notion of a culture of innovation. And, Model S has a particular strategy for assigning tasks to those working on innovation part-time and those doing so full-time. The idea is to get *everyone* involved in innovation, but of course not everyone can be involved *full-time,* because then who would be running the Performance Engine? Therefore, everyone is involved, but only part-time.

As it turns out, Model S is the only one of the three models in which the part-time innovators are the prime movers. Where full-time teams are employed, they take on support roles.

Assigning Innovation Tasks to Part-Time and Full-Time Innovators

Model	Part-Time	Full-Time
S Small	Take initiative Make innovation happen	Provide support

Before considering how to shape these part-time and full-time roles so as to get the most out of Model S, it is worthwhile to examine the inherent constraints that are already evident.

THE LIMITATION TO MODEL S
IS PROJECT SIZE

Model S is very important, and it can be extremely powerful. However, its limitation is not too hard to understand. Put simply, employees are busy. They *already* have full-time jobs. Thus, Model S is an effort to squeeze innovation into the tiny slivers of slack time that exist even in the most efficiently managed organizations.

Doing so is difficult. Imagine that Bob has an idea for improving operations in his department. He's feeling inspired, and he's ready to take some initiative to make things happen. One of the challenges that Bob faces is the threat of constant interruption. Slack time is not reliably available, because few business operations run at a perfect steady state. There are busy weeks and less busy ones. Bob may find that he makes progress for a while, but then has to table his effort as the pressures of day-to-day operations become too great.

If Bob is a persuasive fellow, he can try to convince his friends Mary, Jane, and Jack to join him. Even if Mary, Jane, and Jack are all inspired, however, coordinating their efforts will not be easy. Unless the trio are subject to exactly the same fluctuations in operating tempo as Bob is, the number of potential interruptions just multiply.

Unless all four are willing to get together on nights and weekends, the effort will stall.

It is extremely difficult to aggregate and coordinate more than a few tiny slivers of slack time. *Therefore, the fundamental limitation to Model S is project size.* Any initiative that requires more than a few slivers of slack time is simply too large for Model S.

This limitation, while severe, hardly renders Model S impotent. It is, after all, quite possible to walk a mile by taking fifty thousand tiny steps. Indeed, many organizations have one or more explicit Model S innovation programs in place. These programs go by many names: continuous improvement programs, lean programs, Six Sigma programs, quality programs, knowledge management programs, and so forth.

Because of the limitation, however, it can be crucial to set realistic expectations about what a *culture of innovation* really means. Ambitious employees may inter-

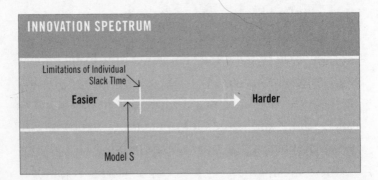

INNOVATION SPECTRUM

Limitations of Individual Slack Time

Easier ← → Harder

Model S

pret it as encouragement to go after major, risky initiatives. Indeed, one of the biggest risks to the ongoing health of Model S is the possibility that it will generate far more ideas than can possibly be implemented. When the reality becomes clear—that for all of the talk about innovation, there is little time for it—the backlash can be severe. Employees may disengage and may lose trust in anything further that they hear from the company about innovation.

Therefore, the messaging with regards to Model S must focus on modest improvements. Yes, everyone can be an innovator, every day. Everyone can come up with ideas, and everyone can even take initiative *by going after small improvements in their immediate areas of responsibility.*

THE KEY TO MODEL S SUCCESS IS MOTIVATION

Model S is heavily reliant on front-line employees going the extra mile. After a long day of work, oftentimes just barely keeping up with the demands of daily business, Model S asks for more. It asks employees to imagine that they have *not just one job but two*: doing the work *and* improving the way the work gets done.

There are many strategies for engaging employees

in Model S. The right approach for a given company depends on its values and its culture. The following options can be used in most any combination; in fact, one company that we studied employed nearly all of them.

1 ▶ *Reinforce individual pride in individual achievement.* This works best in environments in which employees can receive quick and clear feedback on their performance, so they can see the immediate result of their efforts to improve.

2 ▶ *Reinforce collective pride in small improvements.* The mantra: "There is no such thing as a 'small' innovation. Every step matters." Consider events that showcase innovation successes.

3 ▶ *Make visible the connection between innovation and the health of the collective enterprise.* Show that efforts on the front lines lead to performance improvements, more satisfied customers, a growing business, job security, and career growth opportunities for talented employees.

4 ▶ *Create internal competition.* This works best in companies with multiple similar organizational units—a manufacturing company with several similar factories, for example, or a health care sys-

tem with several similar hospitals. Simply sharing the performance of each spurs healthy competition. Which has the lowest costs? The best safety record?

5 ▶ *Have individuals or small teams set performance goals.* Goals motivate, especially when they are self-generated, either by individuals or by small groups that work together each day. Some negotiation of goals with a management team is a good idea, in some cases to raise ambitions, and in others to rein them in a bit to improve the odds of success. Goal setting can backfire if failure is more common than success.

6 ▶ *Encourage peer pressure.* Rather than asking individuals to be responsible for taking initiative, ask small teams that work together every day to be responsible. Have each team post projects and progress visibly in work areas. It will quickly become evident which team members are participating and which are not.

7 ▶ *Make it clear when initiatives are being deferred, not denied.* Performance Engine pressures can be severe, and sometimes front-line supervisors in particular must ensure that day-to-day operations

take priority over innovation. In such times, the motivation to innovate can suffer long-term damage. To offset this risk, make sure that the distinction between "no" and "just as soon as we can" is very clear.

8 ▶ *Pay individuals or small teams for performance.* Set a performance target and pay extra compensation to teams that exceed it. To keep the pressure on, consider regularly increasing the performance target. That way, teams cannot innovate once and collect extra pay indefinitely.

9 ▶ *Penalize only for lack of effort.* Innovation involves risk and experimentation. Not every initiative will succeed. Penalizing someone for trying but failing is deadly to innovation. Therefore, reach for the stick rather than the carrot only when employees refuse to even try.

10 ▶ *Create a system for acknowledging and evaluating big ideas.* These motivational techniques may inspire some big dreaming among some employees. To sustain motivation, it is important that employees feel that such ideas, although too big for Model S, have been heard and will be considered.

PUSHING THE LIMITS OF MODEL S

No matter how good the motivation strategy, however, there are only twenty-four hours in the day. The only way to further increase the output from Model S is to create more slack in the system—which is to say, to deliberately overstaff. For example, Google has become well known for their 20 percent policy, which, in theory, allows some of their employees to spend up to 20 percent of their time in pursuit of whichever ideas inspire them.

Companies have often asked us whether we'd advise that they adopt a similar strategy. Far more often than not, our answer is no. The main reason is that such a policy pushes back the limitation on Model S only a small amount. Even with the 20 percent policy in place, if Bob persuades Mary, Jane, and Jack to join him, we are still talking about an initiative that is consuming less than the equivalent of one full-time employee. We are still talking about very small projects.

So, before embarking on such a policy, ask: Just how meaningful might these small efforts be? Google may deliver a software widget that is valuable, but General Electric is not going to design the next-generation jet engine this way. (If you are thinking that all you hope to do is *start* initiatives through a policy like Google's 20 percent policy, it is worthwhile to think about what fraction you can actually afford to try to finish.)

Furthermore, such a policy is very expensive. If you do the math carefully, you'll see that a 20 percent policy increases human resources costs by 25 percent. Google may find this affordable for a while, but it is out of the question for most companies.

Perhaps the most persuasive argument in favor of a 20 percent policy has only an indirect connection to innovation. The policy may be extremely powerful in recruiting. In software, it is said that the best programmers can be an order of magnitude more productive than the average programmer. If that is true, it may very well be sensible to swallow the cost of the 20 percent policy simply because it makes it possible to recruit those world-class programmers. In most industries, however, the gap between the most productive employees and average ones is measured as a percentage, not a multiple.

There is another approach to pushing the limits of Model S. Instead of deliberately overstaffing to create more slack, consider creating a process to allocate additional resources to employees with particularly compelling ideas that can't be executed on free time alone. In this manner, scarce resources are concentrated where the ideas are most promising, rather than spread indiscriminately throughout the organization.

ROLES FOR THE FULL-TIME TEAMS

Companies sometimes create full-time staffs with responsibility for oversight of Model S innovation programs. These teams go by many names—quality teams, Six Sigma teams, continuous improvement teams, knowledge management teams, and so forth. These teams are often responsible for implementing the motivation strategies described above, being sure to amplify the motivation when the Performance Engine's operating tempo is light and thus slack time is readily available.

They can do more. Especially in larger companies, for example, they can move information and ideas around the company. They might connect people who are working on similar problems so that they can learn from each other. Or, they might help form teams when promising ideas call for collaboration among individuals who do not normally work together. In addition, they can strive to multiply the impact of successful initiatives by looking for other places in the company where they can be repeated.

These teams can also bring analytical firepower to Model S. They may be able to run sophisticated statistical analyses to identify areas where there are rich opportunities for improvement. They might also help with the analytical discipline that is sometimes necessary to determine whether or not an initiative has resulted in a performance improvement for the company.

Perhaps most critically, however, these oversight teams must be sure to redirect Model R or Model C ideas to other innovation channels within the company, rather than letting them stagnate for lack of resources. We turn next to Model R.

CHAPTER 3

MODEL R
DELIVERS REPEATABLE INNOVATION

I f one innovation is good, then a series of similar innovations must be even better. Apple, for example, followed its smashing success with iPhone by launching the iPhone 2, 3, 4, 4S, and 5.

Repeated and predictable innovation success is the ambition underlying Model R. In many industries, there is no way to stay healthy without delivering a steady stream of innovative new offerings. Hasbro delivers hundreds of new toys and games each year. Automakers compete on the strength of new vehicle designs. Movie production houses could hardly remain viable only on the strength of past offerings.

Model R is night-and-day different from Model S.

Creating conditions in which innovation "just happens" organically is the Model S aspiration. Model R, by sharp contrast, is about systematizing innovation. Indeed, the fundamental Model R assumption is that you can treat innovation just like any other business process. You can build a *factory* that delivers innovation in much the same way you build a factory that delivers product.

THE KEY TO MODEL R
SUCCESS IS PROCESS EXCELLENCE

Motivation drives Model S, but *process* is the key to Model R. The fundamental premise is that you can break innovation down into small, discrete, and repeatable tasks. You can script the process, even extensively document it. You can make the process efficient and routine. You can ask people to specialize, performing the same tasks again and again for each subsequent initiative. You can even develop tools for forecasting the time and budget necessary to complete each step, and thus measure every employee's performance and hold each accountable.

With a rigorous Model R process, companies can plan to launch new offerings well in advance. They know exactly what needs to happen day by day in order to ensure nothing gets in the way of a successful launch. Should the work fall behind schedule, the mind-set is to get back on track as quickly as possible, no matter what it takes.

Companies that rely most heavily on Model R are in fast-moving industries that deliver complex, multicomponent products—consumer electronics, appliances, or vehicles, for example. There are so many people involved in developing each new product that their efforts *must* be carefully scripted and coordinated to get the job done.

Many people instinctively imagine that innovation is inherently too unpredictable to be scripted in such a way. While Model R innovations never reach the same levels of repeatability and predictability as other Performance Engine processes, the Model R mind-set is to get as close as possible.

Not all uncertainties can be eliminated. As a result, many companies build *stages and gates* into their Model R processes. If an initiative fails to meet certain specified criteria at each gate, the project may be brought to a halt. The idea is to avoid spending any more than necessary on a project that is headed to failure. Further, almost all Model R projects face significant uncertainties post-launch. Will customers want or not want the new offering? Some new products spread like wildfire, others not at all, and it can be very difficult to predict in advance which are which.

Note, however, that these uncertainties, at each gate and post-launch, relate to *results*—to *outputs* not *inputs*.

By contrast, the inputs—the work steps that need to be executed to get from beginning to end of the initiative—are well understood. And, making the inputs—the sequence of tasks, the people responsible for each, and the time and money required to complete each—as repeatable and predictable as possible is the essence of Model R.

As is true of all three models, one of the defining characteristics of Model R is the logic by which tasks are assigned to those working full-time and those working part-time on innovation. In Model R, part-timers are typically in commercialization roles. They manufacture, market, and sell each new offering, right alongside existing offerings. They work on both innovation and ongoing operations simultaneously. It is the similarity of past, present, and future innovations that makes this possible. The work is much the same for every offering, and thus, the work is easily combined.

Model R full-timers create the innovations. They are designers, engineers, and market researchers, and they typically work in departments with names like new product development, new service development, or new concept development.

In some companies, a separate full-time team is commissioned for each Model R initiative. The design of those teams—especially the hierarchy and the roles, responsibilities, and needed skillsets for each team member—are well established and well understood. It is all part of the script. A design process for new cell phones, for example, might call for a full-time team for each cell phone, with each team composed of one small group of experts focused on analog circuitry, another on digital circuitry, a third focused on radio transmission circuits, and a supervisory group focused on system design.

In other companies, Model R full-timers spread their efforts across several initiatives, perhaps dividing their time between innovations that are in various stages of development. Again, it is the similarity of initiatives that makes this possible.

Specialists in full-time Model R innovation roles generally develop tight-working relationships with other specialists who work on related components of new offerings. For example, at an automaker, you'd expect that the brake designer and the wheel designer would know each other well. These close-working relationships create efficiency, but also, as we will see shortly, rigidity.

Assigning Innovation Tasks to Part-Time and Full-Time Innovators

Model	Part-Time	Full-Time
S Small	Take initiative	Provide support
R Repeatable	Commercialize	Develop

THE LIMITATION TO MODEL R IS PROJECT SIMILARITY

Model R is capable of pushing far beyond the limitations of Model S. Indeed, size is no limitation at all. We studied a routine new product development effort at Deere & Company that cost nearly $100 million—hardly an effort that could be squeezed into little slivers of slack time!

However, for all of Model R's strengths, it is also its own worst enemy. Its drive for efficiency eventually becomes its undoing. *The more efficient a Model R process becomes, the less flexible it becomes.* Indeed, an extremely efficient Model R process is only capable of delivering this year's version of last year's product.

Sometimes, this year's version of last year's product is exactly what is needed. Sometimes, in fact, continually bringing out new and improved versions of existing products is an absolute necessity if you desire to stay ahead of

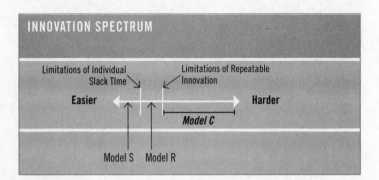

your competition. Where the desire is to serve customers that you already know and understand with ever improved performance in areas that your customers reliably value—and do so repeatedly, predictably, and efficiently—Model R is your friend. It is when you start trying to push outside these boundaries that Model R can become your enemy.

PUSHING THE LIMITS OF MODEL R

As with Model S, it is possible to extend the limits of Model R, but only a little bit. It can be done by recognizing the trade-off inherent in Model R: *efficiency* versus *flexibility*. Thus, to push the limits of Model R a bit, you relax a bit. You allow yourself to be a little bit *less* Performance Engine like. You don't script the process in quite so much detail. You are a bit more forgiving when budgets are exceeded or schedules are revised.

In some cases, you might temporarily relax only selective portions of the process. For example, the Deere effort that we studied was to develop a new, large-scale tractor for industrial agriculture. One of Deere's top goals was to create a fuel-efficiency breakthrough. To do so, they held most of the design team to tight time and budget standards, but deliberately gave the engine design team substantial flexibility. In fact, the management team ultimately chose to accept a six-month delay in the product's launch in order to give the engine team the time it needed to get the job done. The result was exactly what was desired—a 9 percent increase in fuel efficiency that customers cherished.

Recognizing the inherent trade-off between efficiency and flexibility, some companies deliberately leave their Model R innovation process much looser. We've heard some companies say that it would take at least a month of reading to fully understand their innovation process, while others have claimed that their process can be explained with a presentation of just a handful of slides.

RESPECTING THE LIMITS TO MODEL R

That said, Model R has fundamental limitations. The source of these limitations is the people themselves—their skills, the way their roles are defined, their work relationships with each other, and the way they are organized. It is, of course, possible to make changes in these areas, *but not without breaking apart the Model R capability that already exists.*

For example, imagine that you have been developing products for your core customers for decades, and they have always valued one product attribute, let's say *ease of use,* above all else. Your customers don't read owner's manuals, they want to follow their intuition. If anything breaks, they want to be able to troubleshoot and repair quickly and independently. As a result, the product development team is populated primarily of engineers who value simplicity and usability above all else. Indeed, these engineers have been promoted quickly and now fill the most senior roles in product development.

Now imagine that your strategy team has uncovered a promising growth opportunity—an emerging group of customers that is hungry for better options for complex, high-performance products. It's the same product category, but these customers want a much different design. Of course, you have no intention of abandoning your existing customers. You want to serve both.

To succeed, you must recognize that this innovation challenge lies well outside the range of your existing Model R capability. You'll need a team with different areas of expertise. You'll need to define their roles and responsibilities differently. You'll need to rethink the design process, and you'll need to rethink the team's hierarchy. It may be tempting to simply inject some high-performance engineers into your existing team, but doing so might be worse than inefficient. It might harm you in the business you are already in, by diminishing your ability to dazzle your existing customers with simple and intuitive designs.

When you start to sense the need to add people, change the people, change the work relationships between people, or change the hierarchy, you are clearly beyond the limits of Model R. If you are adding new components to your products, rearranging the components physically, creating a new system design that changes how the components connect to each other, aiming to serve a customer that values different attributes of your offering, or dramatically altering the riskiness, magnitude, or duration of the initiative, it is time to move on to Model C.

In fact, Model C is needed even when only a small fraction of the overall design is subject to these types of major changes. For example, we spoke with the team at BMW about their first effort to design a hybrid automobile. For the most part, hybrid automobiles are no different from earlier nonhybrid designs. As such, BMW's extensively documented process for engineering new automobiles was mostly an asset. However, for the hybrid components— brakes, batteries, and engine control—the existing process was a liability. Specialists in these components had never before needed to collaborate. The only way to make it happen was to create a special team. We'll take a second look at this example as we dive deeper into Model C.

CHAPTER 4

MODEL C
IS FOR ALL OTHER INNOVATIONS

F ans of Garrison Keillor, the author and radio show
host, know that his fictional town, Lake Wobegon, is
a place where all of the women are strong, all of the
men are good-looking, and all of the children are above
average. When Keillor first spoke this line, he likely did so
with a sly grin. Of course, it is mathematically impossible
for *all* of the children to be above average.

As a testament to Keillor's popularity, the phrase
"Lake Wobegon Effect" is now commonly used to describe any phenomenon wherein people systematically
overestimate their abilities. (Surveys show that a heavy
majority of managers believe that they are above average
performers.) Psychologists have a more formal name for

this phenomenon: illusory superiority. (No doubt you know at least one person that suffers from illusory superiority.)

So, we wondered if there is also the opposite phenomenon, an "Anti-Lake Wobegon Effect," in which people systematically *under*estimate their abilities. There is, though it is less common. Learning to juggle or to ride a unicycle are good examples. Most anyone, with just a bit of patience and practice, can pick up these circus skills.

We'd add one more item to the Anti-Lake Wobegon effect list: breakthrough innovation. By and large, companies are insecure about how they "rank" against other companies in this area. We're pretty sure that we know who to blame: Apple. This company's marketing machine has been so powerful that many companies seem to be convinced that Apple innovates—and nobody else can.

Let us set the record straight. Apple is a very impressive company, but they do not hold any proprietary secrets on how to manage innovation. And, while they have several impressive innovation victories, they probably wish that they better understood exactly how they did it, so they could do it again and again. While many companies excel at Model S or Model R or both, we believe that no company has, as yet, mastered Model C. All companies "rank" relatively close to one another, in a performance band that could accurately be labeled "ample room for improvement."

Indeed, the nature of our research has *not* been to identify a few supremely talented companies who hold all of the answers (we don't think any exist), and then pick them apart to figure out exactly how they do what they do. Instead, our method has been to study a wide range of examples, both successes and failures, across a wide range of industries, to identify one or two best practices in each example, and then to put together an integrated picture of what it *would* look like if companies *did* get it right consistently.

As we get into Model C terrain, the degree of difficulty is definitely going up. That said, Model C is well within reach for *all* companies. It is a discipline that can be learned.

In fact, there is absolutely nothing that is intellectually complex in the remaining pages of this book. Our recommendations are *easy to understand*. What's hard is *living* them. Performance Engine reflexes get in the way—often without anyone even realizing it. One of the keys to success, therefore, is for all of the executives, managers, and employees who touch Model C initiatives to become keenly aware of the competing priorities. As we will see, each must be surfaced and explicitly resolved.

FIRST, DISPOSE OF THE MYTH

The very first step, however, is to overcome a toxic myth that lives within the hearts and minds of many. In the myth, an inspired visionary has a great idea. Initially, that idea is met with skepticism, but our hero is imbued not just with creativity and insight but also with the determination to make things happen, no matter what gets in the way. Naturally our hero runs into all kinds of barriers. In fact, it seems at times as though the entire organization is trying to fight his progress. No matter. Our hero does what it takes, breaking rules, working underground, nurturing a conspiracy, fighting the system, until *finally,* our hero emerges victorious.

If this sounds silly, that is because it *is* silly. Nonetheless, the myth is alive and well, as reflected by two of the most common questions we get when we give presentations:

1 ▶ How can I identify the true innovators in my organization?

2 ▶ How can I knock down at least a few of the barriers that they will inevitably face?

It would seem that it is completely natural to frame the innovation challenge as a battle between an innovation hero and a bureaucratic octopus. In the real world, however, innovation heroes get strangled, almost every time. Therefore, we need a more productive approach. The "Break All of the Rules" mind-set, no matter how inviting it may seem in books or in the popular press, simply does not work. There are at least three reasons:

1 ▶ *Almost every innovation leader needs the Performance Engine.* After all, it is profits from the Performance Engine that *pay* for innovation. Furthermore, innovation initiatives almost always build on at least something that already exists—a brand, a relationship with customers, or an area of technical expertise, for example.

2 ▶ *"Break All of the Rules" can sound like "Break the Performance Engine."* Think about it. If you are the general manager responsible for being on time, on budget, and on spec every day, every week, and every month, and you hear some young "innovator" say that they are going to "break all of the rules," how are you going to react?

3 ▶ *"Break All of the Rules" can sound like "No Rules."* In our experience, innovators can sound extremely arrogant. "Hey, I'm special. I'm an innovator. I don't have to follow procedure. I'm going to do

things my own way." This attitude just fuels the inevitable tensions with the Performance Engine that easily undermine innovation.

Instead of an antagonistic, "Break All of the Rules" mind-set, what is needed is *mutual respect* between innovation leaders and Performance Engine leaders. To get there, both sides must make a crucial acknowledgment. First, innovation leaders must recognize that *conflict with the Performance Engine is normal*. It is *not* the result of people being lazy or unwilling to change. Quite to the contrary, it is the result of good people doing good work, trying to make the Performance Engine run as efficiently as possible. Performance Engine leaders, for their part, must remember that no Performance Engine lasts forever—or, at least, no Performance Engine grows at double-digit growth rates for very long.

Both sides need the other. There must be mutual respect.

ATTACKING THE FUNDAMENTAL INCOMPATIBILITIES HEAD ON

Mutual respect is a good starting point, but only that. Models S and R both attempt to *work around* the fundamental incompatibilities described in chapter 1. Model S did so by squeezing innovation into the slack in the system; Model R by making innovation look as Performance-Engine-like as possible. To get beyond the limitations to these models, we have no remaining option but to attack the fundamental incompatibilities head on.

The Performance Engine strives for and is organized for repeatability. Innovation, by contrast, is inherently nonroutine. Therefore, we must think very carefully—and very differently—about how we *organize* Model C initiatives. Further, the Performance Engine strives for and is managed based upon a presumption of predictability. Innovation, by contrast, is inherently uncertain. Therefore, we are going to have to think very carefully—and very differently—about how we *plan* Model C initiatives.

There are many contexts in which business people are very comfortable talking about organizing and planning. Somehow, however, these topics are rarely a part of conversations about innovation. The tendency is to get excited about the idea and then simply turn to a leader and say, "Go make it happen!"

To do this, however, is to skip some crucial questions. It is, in fact, to assume that the way the Performance Engine organizes and plans will work for innovation too. This is a fatally flawed assumption. The Performance Engine is powerful, but it is also a highly specialized

FUNDAMENTAL INCOMPATIBILITIES		
Objectives of Ongoing Operations	Repeatability	Predictability
Realities of Innovation	Non-Routine	Uncertain
Can Lead to Challenges in	Organizing	Planning

machine. Model C initiatives take companies well outside of the confines of this specialization.

As such, every Model C initiative needs a *Special Team* and a *Special Plan*. These are the two major components of Model C, and these are the topics we will address in Part II and Part III of this book, respectively.

MATCHING EACH INITIATIVE TO THE RIGHT MODEL

Because Model C is challenging, many companies feel a gravitational pull back to the more familiar and more comfortable models—S and R. Unfortunately, trying to execute a Model C initiative with either Model S or Model R is a quick route to frustration. As such, it is important to have a very firm grasp on methods, challenges, and expected outcomes from each of the three models.

Each Model Presents a
Distinct Managerial Challenge

Model	Strategy for Dealing with the Performance Engine	Central Managerial Challenge
S Small	**Squeeze It In** Squeeze innovation into the slack in the system	Motivation
R Repeatable	**Make It Repeatable and Predictable** Make innovation look as much like day-to-day operations as possible	Process Management
C Custom	**Separate It** Separate incompatible innovation tasks from day-to-day operations	Special Team Special Plan

In particular, it is crucial to understand the limitations of Models S and R. As we have seen, these limits can be pushed, but only a bit. Here are the rules:

1 ▶ *Can the initiative be executed by just a few people, using only their free time?* If yes, use Model S.

You can push the limits of Model S, a bit, by creating more slack in people's schedules and by allocating some additional resources to promising ideas.

2 ▶ *Is the initiative similar enough to a past initiative that the same people in the same roles can follow the same process?* If so, use Model R.

You can push the limits of Model R, a bit, by allowing some flexibility in the process, but watch out for the damage this may do to other initiatives in the pipeline.

3 ▶ *In all other cases, use Model C.* Note that a successful Model C effort might lead to a desire to build a new Model R process for launching a series of new and improved versions of the original innovation. The first iPhone was a Model C effort; each subsequent launch could be managed with Model R.

Consider the following three innovation initiatives from our own industry, business schools.

1 ▶ *Have professors from different disciplines co-teach the same class sessions to help students make connections across the curriculum.* Each co-taught class is a small initiative. This is readily achievable

using only the slack time on professors' schedules. *Verdict:* Model S.

2 ♦ *Develop a new executive education program for CFOs.* Business schools routinely create and market new executive education programs, following a similar process each time. *Verdict:* Model R.

3 ♦ *Develop an online MBA program.* Not only is there no well-understood process for creating such a program, doing so would require hiring at least a small group of new people with specialized expertise in technology for online education, and creating a special team in which these experts worked in close partnerships with faculty. *Verdict:* Model C.

One easy mistake is to allow other innovation categorizations to interfere with your judgment about which model to choose for a given initiative. For example, you may be tempted to only use Model C for innovations you believe are disruptive, not sustaining; or radical, not incremental.

Be careful. These categorizations have more to do with strategy than execution. They are based on what the innovation looks like from the outside, not from the inside.

The criteria for choosing the right model are *internal*. They are tied to the *physics of getting the work done*. We have seen several innovations that few would call disruptive or radical that quite clearly require Model C. For example, Dow Jones made an effort to sell packages of advertisements that crossed all of its media properties—print, online, broadcast, and so forth. Nobody involved imagined that selling bundles of advertisements would turn the industry upside down. Nonetheless, there was no way to execute the initiative without creating a Special Team and a Special Plan.

Model C is the most difficult and the least familiar of the three, but it is also the most robust. Your company will probably need it far more often than you imagine. You may need it for new processes, new products, new services, or new businesses. You may need it for initiatives in most any function.

PART TWO

MODEL C: BUILD THE TEAM

CHAPTER 5

BUILD THE TEAM: AN OVERVIEW

R ecall that every Model C initiative requires a Special Team and a Special Plan. In Part II, we explain the design of the Special Team; in Part III, we will tackle the Special Plan.

There is a crucial transition in thinking that is required as we move from Models S and R to Model C. The first two models, S and R, are both approaches for producing *multiple* innovations. With Model C, we must think one initiative at a time. Each is a *custom* effort. Each requires its own Special Team and Special Plan.

Model C, like the other two models, includes both full-time and part-time innovators. For simplicity, we will refer to full-time members of the Special Team as

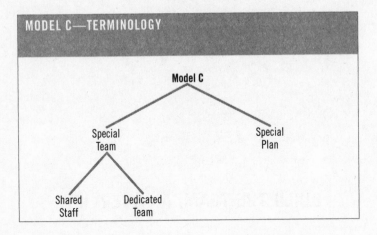

MODEL C—TERMINOLOGY

Model C

Special
Team

Special
Plan

Shared
Staff

Dedicated
Team

the Dedicated Team, and the part-time members as the Shared Staff.

YOU *MUST* CREATE A DEDICATED TEAM FOR *EACH* MODEL C INITIATIVE

Creating a Dedicated Team for each Model C initiative is an absolute necessity. Nonetheless, for many companies, taking this step is one of the most difficult commitments that must be made in pursuit of innovation.

While many companies *do* create full-time teams dedicated to innovation, more often than not these teams focus on the front end of the innovation challenge—on ideas, technology, strategy, and so forth. Here, however, we are talking about something quite different— commissioning a Dedicated Team *to execute a single initiative.* It is an unusual step for many companies, and not a comfortable one.

The fiercest objection to creating a Dedicated Team is usually that doing so is just too expensive. But is it really? Objectively, there is no difference in cost between staffing an initiative that requires five full-time equivalents with five full-time people or with twenty-five people who each contribute one-fifth of their time. Either way, the total number of person-hours expended is the same. The full-time allocation creates greater anxiety in many companies because it is a much more *visible* expense. It shows up easily on someone's internal profit-and-loss statement. Part-time contributions, by contrast, might not be accounted for at all, even though the expense is just as real.

Not only does the creation of a Dedicated Team cost no more, it has powerful advantages. First, when an initiative demands only a small fraction, say 10 percent, of a person's time, it can easily become that person's last priority. It only gets attention once the more pressing 90 percent of the work is complete. In busy times, that 90 percent can expand to 100 percent or more, and the 10 percent allocation quickly shrinks to nothing.

In addition, you can do something crucial with a Dedicated Team that you can't possibly do with part-timers. You can reorganize. You can change people's roles and responsibilities, you can redesign work processes and work relationships, and you can change team structure and team hierarchy. There are no constraints. By contrast, when you have a small fraction of a whole bunch of people's time, it is impossible to reorganize. There already exist clearly defined roles, well-established work relationships, and a firmly entrenched hierarchy. Reorganizing would damage ongoing operations. You can't do it.

For Model C initiatives, being able to reorganize is crucial. *You simply don't get breakthrough innovation without breakthrough organizational design.* This is an axiom we will repeat more than once in the upcoming chapters. And, the only place where breakthrough organizational design is possible is on a Dedicated Team.

There are further issues that come up as soon as you say, "Dedicated Team." Some people, many of whom may be ill-suited for the job, will immediately start angling to be put on such a team, thinking that it sounds exciting, fun, innovative, and potentially career enhancing. Others will immediately run for the hills, worried that being assigned to the team will pose a major career risk if the initiative fails. Some may instinctively wonder whether it is "fair" to create a special team with special rules, while other may insist, "We are one company, with one culture. We don't create special teams that operate differently."

These are all highly predictable emotions and objections, and they do represent potential headaches for leaders. The fact remains, however, that there is simply no way to get beyond the limitations of Models S and R without taking the step of forming custom-designed Dedicated Teams for each Model C initiative.

Note that some companies *do* have a routine habit of creating teams dedicated to single innovation initiatives, but one that is embedded in a Model R innovation process. When this is the case, the teams are not custom designed. Instead, the teams take on the same composition and structure each and every time. The breakthroughs that are possible through Model C can only be reached by going one step further and custom designing each team, from scratch, for the task at hand.

THE DEDICATED TEAM IS NOT THE WHOLE STORY

As important as it is to take the step of commissioning a Dedicated Team, it is not enough to do so. The Special Team is not one group of people, it is two groups. It is a *partnership* between the Dedicated Team and the

Shared Staff. As its name implies, the Shared Staff does double duty. It takes on selected innovation tasks while simultaneously sustaining excellence in day-to-day operations.

Because the Shared Staff remains an integral part of the Performance Engine, it has extremely limited flexibility. Everyone remains in their existing jobs. Everyone continues to report to their existing bosses. Therefore, the Shared Staff can only take on familiar tasks that fit within existing roles and existing work processes. Asking any more is invariably disruptive to ongoing operations.

As such, the Shared Staff can take on *more* work, but never *different* work. As a rule of thumb, if it takes more than a day or two to train the Shared Staff to do the innovation work, it is asking too much. Any tasks that are beyond the reach of the Shared Staff must be handled by the Dedicated Team.

Despite these heavy limitations, the Shared Staff some-

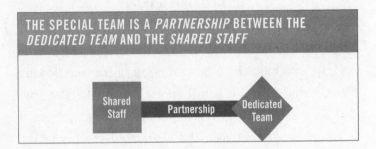

THE SPECIAL TEAM IS A *PARTNERSHIP* BETWEEN THE *DEDICATED TEAM* AND THE *SHARED STAFF*

Shared Staff

Partnership

Dedicated Team

times takes on *most* of the labor. We've seen examples in which the Shared Staff does nearly everything and examples in which the Shared Staff does nearly nothing. It depends on the nature of the innovation work. If most of it is very similar to what the Performance Engine already does, then the Shared Staff can take on most of the work. (We will explore this further in the next chapter.)

Note that we have now seen three different guidelines for assigning the right tasks to the right people, one each for Models S, R, and C.

Assigning Innovation Tasks to Part-Time and Full-Time Innovators

Model	Part-Time	Full-Time
S Small	Take initiative	Provide support
R Repeatable	Commercialize	Develop
C Custom	Familiar tasks Existing workflows Same roles	Unfamiliar tasks New workflows Custom roles

THE DEDICATED TEAM HAS NEARLY
UNLIMITED FLEXIBILITY

In sharp contrast to the Shared Staff, the Dedicated Team faces almost no organizational design constraints. Indeed, the right mind-set when building the Dedicated Team is to imagine you are building a new company from the ground up.

In the diagram, note that the Dedicated Team is represented by a diamond while the Shared Staff, like the Performance Engine, is represented by a square. It is as though we have literally taken the square and turned it on its side. Done properly, the Dedicated Team faces only the constraints faced by start-ups, such as whom you are able to recruit.

Building the Dedicated Team as though you are building a new company from scratch implies hiring new people with new skills, creating titles and job descriptions from a blank page, designing a hierarchy and organizational structure from scratch, and even differentiating, to a degree, the culture of the Dedicated Team from that of the Performance Engine. None of this is easy to do. In fact, one of the most common errors that we have observed in our research is the construction of Dedicated Teams that act no differently from the rest of the organization. We call these *Little Performance Engines*.

Let's reconsider the axiom: *You don't get break-through innovation without breakthrough organizational design.* While it is crucial to practice breakthrough organizational design when building the Dedicated Team, it is important to note that such redesign is necessary *only* within the Dedicated Team. It is *not* necessary to tamper with the structure of the Shared Staff. It is *not* necessary to redesign the entire company. Indeed, the goal is to leave the Performance Engine untouched and unharmed.

IT'S NOT A PEACEFUL PARTNERSHIP

For the Special Team to be effective, the Dedicated Team and the Shared Staff must work in harmony. This is hardly guaranteed. First, the conflicts between innovation and ongoing operations are constant. Second, if you build the Dedicated Team properly—if you turn the square into the diamond—then what you have is two very different groups trying to get along. It's like Mars trying to get along with Venus.

All of this said, to give up on the partnership is to give up on innovation itself. You *must* make the partnership work, despite the fact that it is inevitably a difficult one.

Making it work, first and foremost, takes the right kind of leadership. The innovation leader must be someone who wants to partner with the Performance Engine, not fight it. And, senior level engagement is crucial, because many common conflicts can only be resolved at the top.

Finally, understaffing the Shared Staff is deadly to the partnership. The Shared Staff *must* have adequate capacity to do both of its jobs. Keep in mind that yesterday the Shared Staff had one job, ongoing operations; today it has two, ongoing operations plus innovation. As such, the Shared Staff typically needs to expand.

As simple as this sounds, it is often overlooked. Even if the Shared Staff is initially able to handle the added workload using only its slack time, additional hiring might be needed as the initiative starts succeeding and growing. As Performance Engines are generally quite facile with growth, this is typically not a problem—as long as the need is recognized.

AVOID COMMON ERRORS

In the next three chapters, we will break down the process of building the special kind of team into three steps.

1 ▶ Divide the Labor (between the Shared Staff and the Dedicated Team)

2 ▶ Assemble the Dedicated Team

3 ▶ Manage the Partnership

Even at the higher level of description in this chapter, however, there are at least six common mistakes.

COMMON ERROR #1
FAILING TO CREATE A DEDICATED TEAM

Performance
Engine

1 ▶ *Failing to Create a Dedicated Team.* Model S and Model R have sharp limits that must be respected. The only way beyond these limits is to create custom-designed, dedicated teams for each initiative.

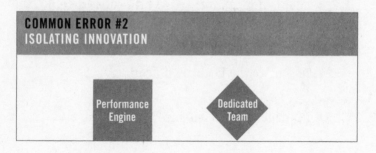

COMMON ERROR #2
ISOLATING INNOVATION

Performance Engine

Dedicated Team

2 ▶ *Isolating Innovation.* Responding to the deep conflicts between innovation and ongoing operations,
some companies choose to put the Dedicated Team
in a faraway place with no contact with the rest of
the company. Such "skunk works" operations can
sometimes be effective in the front end of innovation, but they are of little use in execution. When
established companies choose this model, they
forfeit the one and only advantage they have
over start-ups: the ability to leverage Performance Engine assets, such as a brand or relationships with customers.

COMMON ERROR #3
BREAKING THE PERFORMANCE ENGINE

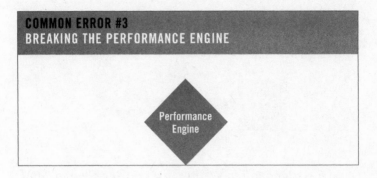

3 ▶ *Breaking the Performance Engine.* We've received a few calls from potential clients who have said they are frustrated with their company's innovation efforts and are contemplating a radical reorganization of the entire company. As much as we believe that you can't get breakthrough innovation without breakthrough organizational design, this is going way overboard. If ongoing operations are running well, then leave the Performance Engine alone. Breakthrough organizational design is necessary, but it can be contained within the Dedicated Team.

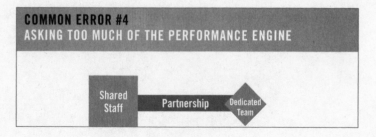

4 ▶ *Assigning Too Many Tasks to the Shared Staff.*
The Shared Staff is already in place, while the
Dedicated Team must be built from scratch. As a
result, when it is unclear which group a task
should be assigned to, the gravitational pull is toward the Shared Staff. It seems quicker and easier.
Unfortunately, this is an area where instincts
lead you astray. The Shared Staff is highly constrained. Asking too much of it can be deadly.
When in doubt, assign the work to the Dedicated
Team.

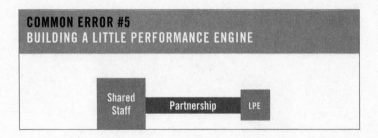

COMMON ERROR #5
BUILDING A LITTLE PERFORMANCE ENGINE

Shared Staff — Partnership — LPE

5 ▶ *Building a Little Performance Engine.* The Dedicated Team must be built from a clean slate—as a diamond, not a square. To get there, all assumptions and all organizational norms must be thoroughly questioned. *Who is on the team? What roles will they fill? Who will they report to?* Unless these questions are addressed without any reference to precedent, the likely result is not a healthy Dedicated Team but a Little Performance Engine.

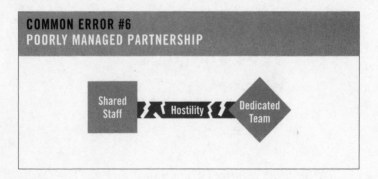

6 ▶ *Poorly Managed Partnership.* A neglected partnership quickly deteriorates. Keeping the partnership healthy requires active engagement from senior executives.

CHAPTER 6

DIVIDE THE LABOR

Quite intuitively, the very first step in building the partnership is deciding what each partner will be responsible for. Which tasks will the Dedicated Team take on and which will the Shared Staff handle?

This is not a complicated idea, but the consequences of getting it wrong are high. Even when the division of labor is perfectly appropriate, the partnership between Dedicated Team and the Shared Staff is delicate. Demand too much of the Shared Staff and the partnership becomes impossible. The opposite error, asking too little of the Shared Staff, is less common and less deadly, but it does dampen an established company's one major advantage over start-ups—its ability to build on what already exists.

As described in the previous chapter, the rule for dividing the labor, when boiled down to its essence, is simple enough. You can ask the Shared Staff to do *more* work, but you cannot ask the Shared Staff to do *different* work.

How different is too different? If it takes more than a day on two of training to get the Shared Staff up to speed, then it's too different. If it doesn't fit naturally in existing work processes, then it's too different. If the members of the Shared Staff can't stay within their existing roles, as currently defined, then it's too different.

What we will do in this chapter is dig a little bit deeper. We'll show the underlying logic for why the Shared Staff is so heavily constrained and offer some additional guidelines and examples.

WHEN THE STRENGTH OF A TEAM IS *LESS THAN* THE SUM OF THE INDIVIDUALS WITHIN IT

Any sports fan has heard the maxim: "The team is greater than the sum of the individuals within it." In most every context we can think of, we like that maxim. For example, it is absolutely true for the Dedicated Team.

It is completely wrong, however, for the Shared Staff. The simple reason is that the Shared Staff *already has a job to do*—excelling at ongoing operations. It's a demanding job, and there's no letup. The Shared Staff can't break away from it.

One of the reasons that companies ask too much of the Shared Staff is that they look at the enormous talents of the individuals within the Shared Staff and imagine that they could do anything! What's critical to realize is that these individuals have already been organized for a very specific purpose—the day-to-day work of the Performance Engine. Everyone has been given a narrowly defined role, and well-established processes move the work from one person to the next; on time, on budget, and on spec.

This may deliver consistent results, but it also creates severe limitations, and you can see them in teams as small as just two people. Think about someone you've worked with for a long time. You know her well, she knows you well. The division of work is clear. You know exactly what to expect from her, she knows exactly what to expect from you. You know the types of decisions that she's in charge of, and vice versa. You know exactly what information she'll share with you routinely, and vice versa.

Now imagine that the two of you were given a completely new and unfamiliar assignment. It's one that will require that you rethink and renegotiate your work relationship from scratch. Maybe even the balance of power will shift dramatically. Maybe you've always worked for her, but in the new assignment she'll be working for you.

Bringing about a dramatic change in work relationships, even in groups of just two people, is hard work. Now imagine trying to do so *while simultaneously sustaining excellence in the work you already do.* It's nearly impossible. Every day, the existing work reinforces the relationship that's already in place.

If you could pull the Shared Staff away from its responsibilities for day-to-day operations, *then* it is at least *possible* to break down the team and reassemble it. You could redefine roles, responsibilities, and hierarchy. You could reshape the work relationships between each pair of individuals on the team.

By doing so, you might be able to convert a team that designed tractors into one that designs locomotives. You might turn a sales team that excelled at closing small transactional sales every day into one that works more methodically toward bigger sales every month. You might be able to transform a consumer-oriented marketing team into one that is effective in reaching business buyers. *But you'd have no hope at doing any of this without first <u>removing</u> the day-to-day pressures that the team already faces.*

Think about it. Not even the world's most talented eleven athletes could *simultaneously* play soccer and (American) football. The thought is, on the surface, laughable. That said, many companies make the mistake of imagining that the Shared Staff's only constraint is the individual skills of the people within it. The folly is exactly the same. No matter how talented the individuals are, the Shared Staff's capabilities are narrow. They are limited by the way the team is organized—and you *cannot* change the way the Shared Staff is organized without inflicting damage on the Performance Engine.

SOME ADDITIONAL GUIDELINES
FOR DIVIDING THE LABOR

Because of the limitations imposed on the Shared Staff by the demands of ongoing operations, it is best, when in doubt, to assign work to the Dedicated Team. In particular, avoid asking the Shared Staff to:

1 ▶ *Reorganize.* All tasks that require new roles or new workflows must be assigned to the Dedicated Team.

2 ▶ *Shift power.* If executing the innovation initiative is consistent with existing workflows but shifts the balance of power between two individuals or two small groups, the work performed by *both*

individuals or small groups must be assigned to the Dedicated Team. It is unrealistic to expect Bob to work for Mary for Performance Engine work, but Mary to work for Bob for simultaneous innovation work. When appliance maker Electrolux chose to enter the luxury end of the market, they created a Dedicated Team in which market researchers and designers were most powerful. These functions could never have been as powerful within the company's engineering-driven Performance Engine.

3 ▶ *Develop new collaborations.* If executing the innovation initiative requires a pair of individuals or a pair of small groups who are unfamiliar with each other to develop a new, in-depth work relationship to perform nonroutine and uncertain innovation work, it is almost always unrealistic to expect this to happen within the confines of the Performance Engine. There is generally insufficient slack and inadequate flexibility in the system to allow it. As such, the work performed by both parties should be shifted to the Dedicated Team. For example, BMW's progress in designing its first hybrid automobile accelerated when it created a Dedicated Team that brought together brake specialists, battery specialists, and engine

control specialists for their first-ever close collaboration.

4 ▶ *Work at two different operating tempos.* If some of the innovation work proceeds at a much different operating rhythm than Performance Engine work, it is almost always better to shift this work to the Dedicated Team. For example, it can be very difficult to get a fast-paced Performance Engine (say, a hospital emergency room) to prioritize long-rhythm tasks (say, a multiyear clinical trial).

5 ▶ *Add new hires.* If you are hiring new people with new skills for the specific purpose of executing the innovation initiative, put those people on the Dedicated Team. Outsiders are extremely important on the Dedicated Team—we'll see why in the next chapter—and giving them Performance Engine responsibilities will only diminish their effectiveness.

The Shared Staff faces sharp constraints. That said, assigning appropriate innovation work to the Shared Staff can be extremely powerful. It saves time, saves money, and takes advantage of an established corporation's biggest advantage—their existing assets.

It is worthwhile, however, to note that the ability to assign work to a Shared Staff is *least* valuable when the asset that is being "borrowed" is completely embodied by a single person, as opposed to a team, a work process, an information technology system, or an intangible asset like a brand. In such situations, it is generally clearer and more effective to simply move that person to the Dedicated Team. For example, consider a company with a small graphic design department within which the individual designers are accustomed to working independently. If an innovation initiative had enough work to justify a full-time graphic designer, why not assign the designer to the Dedicated Team? If nothing is lost by shifting the work from the Shared Staff to the Dedicated Team, then it is better to do so.

WHEN MODELS R AND C OVERLAP

Figuring out how to properly divide the labor between the Dedicated Team and the Shared Staff can be confusing when the Shared Staff is a new product development or new service development team. In such situations, Model R and Model C overlap on the organizational chart. The Shared Staff works simultaneously on Model R and Model C innovations.

That said, our earlier observations about the limitations of Model R and our earlier warnings about work that should *not* be assigned to the Shared Staff still apply. Be sure to recognize:

1 ▸ When a company's Model R process churns out product after product based on the same system design, that system design becomes embedded in the product development team's process and organizational model. Therefore, any system redesign will lead to the need to create a new workflow and to reorganize the specialists. Such changes can only happen on a Dedicated Team.

2 ▸ When a company transitions from offering *components* to offering *custom solutions,* a Dedicated Team is needed to handle systems design, but component designs can still be handled by the Shared Staff.

3 ▸ When a company seeks to serve a new customer set with different priorities (say, a new customer that values design over engineering performance, like the Electrolux example mentioned earlier in this chapter), a Dedicated Team is needed that shifts the balance of power between engineering specialties, adding power to those

who specialize in what the new customers most value.

4 ♦ Breakthrough new product designs often take much longer than routine ones, perhaps several years instead of several months. Such long-rhythm efforts can be endlessly deferred within product development organizations that are constantly under pressure to launch new products. Such efforts are best assigned to a Dedicated Team.

CHAPTER 7

ASSEMBLE THE DEDICATED TEAM

In the prior chapter, we analyzed which tasks the Shared Staff could tackle while simultaneously sustaining excellence in ongoing operations. Every remaining task must be assigned to the Dedicated Team.

Only the Dedicated Team can accommodate the breakthrough organizational design that is so critical to Model C innovation. The Dedicated Team must be built as though you are building a new company from the ground up. There are three steps:

1 ▶ First, list the skills the Dedicated Team needs to get its work done. It's very important to start with *skills you need* rather than *people you know*.

2 ▶ Second, hire the best people you can possibly get *from any source,* whether internal transfers, new hires, or even acquisitions of small companies. Prioritize people who have the specific skills needed to get the work done over people who are "innovative."

3 ▶ Finally, develop an organizational model—roles, hierarchy, culture—that is *customized to the task at hand.*

There is not much more that can be said about what a *particular* Dedicated Team should look like. There are an infinite number of innovation initiatives, and thus an infinite number of possible designs for the Dedicated Team. It is impossible to generalize.

We can, however, say a great deal about what to avoid. Above all else, you do *not* want to build a Little Performance Engine, a small team that behaves just like the rest of the company.

Even though the Dedicated Team, in theory, faces no constraints, it is difficult to truly act as though you are building a new company from scratch when you work within an established company. As we will see, there are dozens of instincts and pressures that will push you to do the wrong thing.

We've seen it in case study after case study. All too

easily, companies slip into the Little Performance Engine trap. They fail to do enough to turn the square into the diamond. In the remainder of this chapter, therefore, we take a much closer look at five specific mistakes that create the problem.

MISTAKE #1: TOO MANY INSIDERS

It is generally easier, faster, and more comfortable to move insiders onto the Dedicated Team than it is to recruit outsiders with new skills. Doing the latter can be cumbersome. It can require working with new search firms or relying on personal networks rather than the company's established recruiting channels.

That said, too great a fraction of insiders on the Dedicated Team can be problematic. The most direct issue that it can create is a skills shortfall. If, for example, a manufacturing company desires to expand the value it offers its customers by launching new services, it probably makes sense to hire a few people from those specific service industries. This logic is straightforward, but the pressures to move quickly are high, and the tendency to overestimate the skills of the people you already have is commonplace.

Dedicated Teams that are dominated by insiders are

also far more likely to act like Little Performance Engines. Part of the reason is that insiders tend to share, and mutually reinforce, a common set of assumptions about what leads to business success. These are, of course, the factors that are believed to have been important in driving the Performance Engine's past successes—and they may or may not have anything to do with what matters for the innovation initiative.

Even more perniciously, Dedicated Teams composed entirely of insiders, especially those who know each other and have worked together in the past, typically struggle to adapt to a new organizational model. Consider two people who have worked closely for a long time within the Performance Engine. Despite the new demands of the innovation initiative, their work relationship is likely to persist on the Dedicated Team—the same assumptions about who does what work, who is in charge, what information is shared, and so forth. Work relationships are sticky.

We argued in the last chapter that changing a work relationship within the Shared Staff is next to impossible. It is, thanks to the relentless pressures of day-to-day operations, which constantly reinforce the existing relationship. Redefining work relationships is far more feasible within the Dedicated Team, *but it remains hard.* It still requires a very explicit and conscious effort on the part of both parties to reconsider and renegotiate the relationship with the innovation initiative in mind. (It may help to think about your spouse. How easy is it to renegotiate this long-standing work relationship—who does what, who makes which decisions, and so on?)

The larger the Dedicated Team, the greater the effort required to overcome the inertia of past work relationships. Every relationship has to be renegotiated. Each one that is *not* renegotiated is like an anchor dragging the team toward a not-so-desirable status as a Little Performance Engine.

The solution? Outsiders. They naturally counter each of the three problems described above. They bring new skills. They naturally challenge assumptions, simply because they have experienced a different history of success and failure. Most critical, however, is that outsiders are natural catalysts in *breaking down existing work relationships and building new ones from scratch.* It's easier for them. They don't have any prior work relationships to break down.

The most powerful predictor of a company's ability to turn the square into the diamond—to avoid the Little Performance Engine problem—is the fraction of outsiders on the team. As one CEO put it to us, "If you want to change the culture, change the people." Exactly right. It is hard to make a quantitative prescription, but we get anxious when the proportion of outsiders is less than one in four. (As we will see in the next chapter, it is possible to go too far. You also need insiders on the Dedicated Team to help navigate the inevitably challenging partnership with the Shared Staff.)

MISTAKE #2: DEFAULTING TO EXISTING JOB DEFINITIONS

If you go the extra mile and do a great job picking the right team members, including plenty of outsiders, but then take a shortcut and simply recycle the same old titles and job descriptions, you still might get a Little Performance Engine. Titles and job descriptions don't get enough respect—at least in the context of forming Dedicated Teams. A title can be much more than words on a business card, especially in the confines of an established company. It says a lot about what you do, what authority you have, and how others in the company relate to you. These are exactly the understandings that you want to *undo* when you build a Dedicated Team.

So, why not make up completely new titles? That way, when members of the Dedicated Team meet each other for the first time, they will be less likely to assume that they already understand what each person's role is. Instead, they'll ask questions and start highly productive conversations about how the team will operate and what each person's role within it will be. The process of rewriting job descriptions may sound like a formality to some, but going through the exercise also helps stimulate the process of breaking down and reshaping work relationships.

There is at least one other step that helps break down and reform new work relationships: giving the Dedicated Team its own physical space. Even in an era of Internet video calls and "virtual organizations," intense face-to-face interaction remains valuable, especially when bringing a new team together.

MISTAKE #3: LEAVING THE SAME PEOPLE IN CHARGE

There is one specific attribute of work relationships that is by far the most difficult to change: *Who is in charge?* People like to hold on to power. If you've worked for the same boss for many years, for example, it will be very awkward for that person to then turn around and work for you on a Dedicated Team.

Shifting the balance of power, however, between people or between functions, is often crucially important for innovation initiatives. The New York Times Company's launch of its Internet unit, New York Times Digital (NYTD), is a useful case in point. Because NYTD does very little of its own journalism (it gets most of its content from *The New York Times* and other third parties), it is really best thought of as an Internet media company. Indeed, it has more in common with Yahoo! than its parent company. As such, it only makes sense that Internet media experts, not senior journalists and editors, should be perched at the top of NYTD's pecking order. This is, of course, exactly the opposite of what makes sense for the newspaper, where senior journalists are at the top and IT professionals are clearly in support roles. Early in NYTD's history, however, the newspaper's hierarchy persisted. NYTD's progress accelerated only when it hired a massive number of Internet experts from the outside. In time, the hierarchy flipped.

The necessary power shift can be achieved in part through formal means, such as decision rights spelled out on job descriptions. It can also be achieved by choosing the right people for the most powerful roles. The leader's background, for example, greatly influences which of the core functions dominates decision making on the Dedicated Team.

MISTAKE #4: ADOPTING THE SAME METRICS, PROCESSES, OR CULTURE

People, roles, and hierarchy are the most powerful shapers of the Dedicated Team's behavior, but there are others. If the Dedicated Team instinctively watches the same measures of performance that the Performance Engine watches (or, worse, calculates bonuses based on them), it will replicate its behaviors. If it takes a shortcut and recycles process maps from the Performance Engine, it will replicate its behaviors. And, if it gives little thought to how its culture may need to be differentiated from that of the Performance Engine, it will replicate its behaviors.

Leaders of Dedicated Teams are often eager to create a distinct culture, but then stumble when doing so. One common mistake is to try to define the Dedicated Team's culture with words like innovative, creative, or fast-moving. Doing so may help attract people to the Dedicated Team, but there is a caustic side effect. The Performance Engine will not like the implication that it shares none of these attributes. Such resentments can easily undermine the critical partnership between the Dedicated Team and the Shared Staff.

Therefore, any effort to define a distinct culture for the Dedicated Team should focus not on "innovativeness" but on the specifics of how the Dedicated Team's *work* is different. Consider, for example, a company that has a history of selling low-priced but reliable products to value-conscious consumers. If this company were to launch an innovation effort aimed at reaching well-heeled consumers with high-performance products, the Dedicated Team's culture would best celebrate not inventiveness in general, but the invention of exotic features that these customers love.

MISTAKE #5: DEFAULTING TO THE SAME POLICIES

Functions like human resources, finance, accounting, and information technology are often referred to as "support functions." This diminishing term may lead many to underappreciate just how powerful these functions can be in shaping the behavior of Dedicated Teams. After all, they have tremendous sway over the topics we've touched upon so far in this chapter, such as hiring processes, titles, job descriptions, metrics, and process definitions.

In order to turn the square into a diamond, these functions *must be willing to differentiate their policies for Dedicated Teams*. Unfortunately, these functions, by and large, want to keep things simple. Particularly if they are under pressure to cut costs, the easiest thing to do is to insist on a common set of policies for the entire company. Doing so also seems egalitarian and fair to everyone in the company.

Sadly, one-size-fits-all policy-making is deadly to Dedicated Teams. It is the superhighway to the Little Performance Engine problem.

Creating distinct policies for the Dedicated Team may ruffle feathers—especially creating separate compensation policies. Doing so, however, is often necessary in order to recruit the best possible people. When recruiting outsiders with new and unfamiliar skills, the relevant compensation benchmark is the market rates for these skills, not the current compensation for the insiders with the most nearly related skillset.

Internal transfers may also want to be compensated differently when accepting a position on the Dedicated Team. They might even angle for the enormous upside potential that might be possible if they joined a similar venture-capital-backed start-up—but that's asking for far too much. Corporate entrepreneurs suffer little of the personal financial risk and unemployment risk that start-up entrepreneurs accept. As such, adjusting career incentives is generally more reasonable than making major adjustments to compensation. If the initiative succeeds, it can and should be a fast track to advancement; if it does not, it can delay but should not kill your career. It's important that participation on a Dedicated Team is never a career killer. If this year's innovation initiative destroys someone's career, nobody will sign up for next year's.

CHAPTER 8

MANAGE THE PARTNERSHIP

The partnership between the Dedicated Team and the Shared Staff is challenging. As such, the first piece of guidance for innovation leaders is: Don't make the problem any more difficult than it already is. *Never antagonize the Performance Engine.*

Indeed, the best innovation leaders that we have witnessed immediately discharge any notion that they can win by "fighting the system." They understand that the Performance Engine is a partner, not an enemy. They don't imagine that their innovation initiative, important though it may be, is the "future of the company." They never think of the Performance Engine as the "aging dinosaur," and they certainly never let any of their team members voice such toxic sentiments. Instead, they go way out of their way to build the partnership on positive terms. They never miss an opportunity to share credit with the Shared Staff.

It would be nice if a collaborative spirit, positive energy, and kindness were enough to assure a healthy partnership. Alas, the conflicts between innovation and ongoing operations are sufficiently intense that even the best innovation leaders need help from above. In this chapter, we outline three critical roles for senior leaders.

1 ❯ To actively adjudicate operational conflicts

2 ❯ To ensure that the Shared Staff is adequately resourced

3 ❯ To anticipate and mitigate tensions in the partnership

IT'S NEVER A FAIR FIGHT

The generic organization chart below is useful for illustrating why innovation leaders need help. On the right, you'll see the innovation leader, the full-time manager with greatest responsibility for the overall success of the initiative. Both the Dedicated Team and the Shared Staff report directly to this leader.

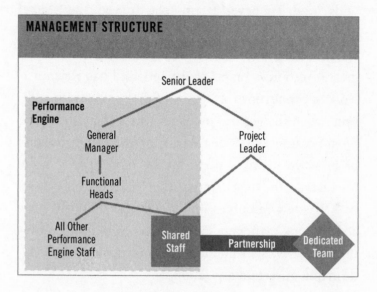

However, because the Shared Staff also retains its responsibilities for ongoing operations, it also reports to the existing chain of command, perhaps to a functional leader, then a general manager, then a senior executive. (Although the org chart shows just one, Dedicated Teams often partner with multiple Shared Staffs in different functions or different business units. The approach to managing these partnerships remains the same; the time and energy required to manage them goes up.)

Because we know that innovation and ongoing operations are inevitably in conflict, we know that the innovation leader and the general manager are going to be at odds. And, it's never a fair fight. Indeed, the general manager wins roughly 100 percent of the time.

After all, the general manager is more senior, has far greater resources under command, and has a rich network of connections at the top of the company. In addition, when the general manager wants something, it is often because a customer wants it *right now* or because of pressure to hit a performance target *this quarter*. Meanwhile, the typical innovation leader is relatively junior, has few resources under command, and has few connections at the top. Furthermore, when the innovation leader wants something, it is in pursuit of a long-term and uncertain aspiration.

Some senior executives make the error of thinking, "Hey, you two are adults! Work it out!" Unfortunately, this is akin to imagining that the hammer and the nail can work out their differences. A determined Performance Engine smashes innovation, every time.

To give the innovation initiative a reasonable chance at survival there must be an *even more powerful force* in the mix—one or more senior executive sponsors who are able and willing to prioritize innovation over ongoing operations when doing so is in the company's long-term best interest. To be effective, this executive needs to understand that routinely adjudicating the conflicts that arise between innovation and ongoing operations is a critical job. It is also time-consuming, but without this investment of valuable senior executive time, dollars spent on innovation are dollars wasted.

It is also important that this executive understand that doing the job well typically requires getting involved in operational issues that are normally well below the radar screens of senior executives. In one of the companies we studied, a chief operating officer had to visit a factory floor to resolve a dispute about whether production starts would be allocated to Performance Engine products or a new product. These allocation decisions were normally made by factory floor managers based on a policy that favored the most profitable and established products. Without the intervention from the top, innovation had no chance.

We are often asked just how senior this executive must be, or, put another way, just how high must the innovation leader report? The answer is, high enough to reach a senior executive that can consistently take a long-term view on what is best for the company. In one case we studied, the innovation leader reported to a board member.

Depending on how terms like "general manager" and "functional heads" are used in a particular company, it can be difficult to interpret the generic organizational chart (see p. 97). It may sometimes be appropriate for the innovation leader to report to someone with a general manager title. The key consideration is how that general manager's performance is evaluated. If nearly all of what matters is whether or not the general manager's quarterly operations are on time, on budget, and on spec, then the innovation leader needs to report higher still.

As a general rule of thumb, the innovation leader needs to report at least two levels higher in the hierarchy than his or her budget would suggest. This can be awkward, especially in companies wherein people equate status with position on the org chart. Awkward or not, this reporting structure is absolutely essential.

ENSURE THAT THE SHARED STAFF HAS SUFFICIENT CAPACITY FOR BOTH JOBS

Yesterday, the Shared Staff had just one job: ongoing operations. Today, it has two: ongoing operations plus an innovation initiative. Therefore, wouldn't it make sense to add people to the Shared Staff?

As obvious as this sounds, the need to scale up the Shared Staff is often overlooked. The consequences to the partnership are devastating. When the Shared Staff has too much to do, it almost inevitably prioritizes ongoing operations. That's generally the much larger of its two jobs, the one with nearer-term deadlines, and the one that matters most on individual performance reviews.

Several steps can be taken to ensure that the Shared Staff has adequate capacity to do both of its jobs well:

1 ▶ *Coordinate budgeting.* Sometimes, the problem is that the budget for the Shared Staff and that of the Dedicated Team are made independently of each other. The innovation initiative needs a budgeting forum in which *all* of the resources necessary for success can be approved or denied.

2 ▶ *Insist that the innovation leader pay for what he or she gets from the Shared Staff.* This requires creating some sort of internal accounting transfer. Doing so is well worth the trouble. Once this payment is in place, the Performance Engine leader no longer sees his or her bottom line diminished because he or she is supporting an innovation initiative. Also, the payment, even if the specific amount is just an estimate, changes attitudes. Suddenly, the innovation initiative looks less like a distraction and more like a customer.

3 ▶ *Adjust the Shared Staff's performance metrics.* This is particularly worthwhile if the Shared Staff is assessed based on its capacity utilization. The innovation leader faces much greater uncertainty than exists in the Performance Engine.

He or she might bulk up on Shared Staff resources in anticipation of high demand that does not materialize. Shared Staff leaders should not be penalized for this. Their results should be isolated from the uncertainty of the innovation initiative wherever possible.

4 ▶ *Create special incentives for the Shared Staff.* One way to increase the capacity of the Shared Staff is to motivate it to work harder or work longer hours. Special performance targets, rewards, or incentives, possibly compensation related, might stimulate the desired behavior. An explicit addition to individual performance reviews, specifically calling out people's willingness and energy in supporting the innovation initiative, may do the same.

NEUTRALIZING ANXIETIES
THAT UNDERMINE THE PARTNERSHIP

Even with the right type of innovation leader, active adjudication of conflicts from senior levels, and an adequately resourced Shared Staff, there are still plenty of sources of tension in the partnership. Among the most difficult to contend with are those that relate to concrete business concerns. Sometimes, an innovation initiative has the potential to harm the existing business. It may cannibalize Performance Engine sales, for example, with a lower-priced offering. Or, if the innovation initiative goes awry, a company's well-regarded brand could be damaged.

These are strategic considerations that are well outside the scope of this book. Sometimes it makes sense to cannibalize your own products, especially if a rival might soon cannibalize you. Sometimes the risk to the brand is acceptable, and sometimes the brand can be protected by creating distinct sub-brands.

Regardless of the rationale, once senior executives commit to the innovation initiative, it is crucial that they communicate why the risks of cannibalization or brand damage are sensible, and what steps are being taken to mitigate the risks. A Shared Staff that is not comfortable with or does not understand the strategy has ample opportunity to undermine it.

A variety of other factors can contribute to an "us-versus-them" environment that subverts an otherwise healthy partnership. Tensions are generally grounded in ways that the Dedicated Team is different from the rest of the company or is treated differently. Maybe the Dedicated Team is compensated differently, or its performance is assessed differently, or the expectations placed on it appear more forgiving. Maybe the Dedicated Team is perceived as "the future" and others are jealous. Alternatively, the Dedicated Team might be perceived as a "quirky experiment" and deemed irrelevant.

The best way to deal with these tensions is for senior executives to address them head on, explaining that the differences between the Dedicated Team and the rest of the company were created purposefully and are necessary to have a legitimate shot at innovation success. Most critically, the senior team must communicate that everyone is part of the same company, and that the company's long-term vitality depends on success at *both* innovation and ongoing operations.

Creating at least some degree of familiarity and similarity between the Dedicated Team and Shared Staff can also help smooth these types of tensions. For all of the emphasis we placed on outside hires in the preceding chapter, insiders on the Dedicated Team make the partnership smoother, especially when they are put into the jobs that require the most direct and frequent interaction with the Shared Staff. When practical, locating the Dedicated Team physically near the Shared Staff, so as to make face-to-face interaction convenient, can also help. Finally, even though the Dedicated Team may have a culture that is purposefully distinct from that of the Performance Engine, there are, no doubt, some values that both partners share—at the very least, basic virtues like teamwork and integrity. Reinforcing common values can strengthen the partnership.

PART THREE

MODEL C: CREATE THE PLAN

CHAPTER 9

CREATE THE PLAN: AN OVERVIEW

In Part III, we lay out a methodology for *planning* a Model C initiative. The Special Plan, recall, is the response to the second of the two fundamental incompatibilities between ongoing operations and innovation. While the Performance Engine strives for *predictability* in everything it does, innovation is by nature *uncertain*. This demands that we think very differently about how we plan and evaluate innovation initiatives.

Let's start with an obvious observation: *Every innovation initiative is properly regarded as an experiment.* And, in one sense, it is easy to run an experiment. Just go try something new!

However, when large amounts of money are at stake, "just going and trying something" is irresponsible at best.

The alternative is to run a *disciplined experiment*, and the payoff is enormously valuable: Quick learning.

In this chapter, we outline the foundational principles for disciplined experimentation. We discuss: 1) why learning matters most, 2) why intuition is inadequate to ensure learning, and 3) how Performance Engine planning systems get in the way.

LEARNING FIRST, PROFITS SECOND

We believe that in the context of innovation initiatives, learning is so valuable that it should be prioritized over results. This contention, as you might imagine, is often met with instinctive and sometimes sharply worded resistance. Prioritizing literally anything over results can be anathema inside the Performance Engine, where the emphasis is always on time, on budget, and on spec. Furthermore, learning sounds like such a soft, amorphous, and difficult-to-assess objective.

Therefore, let us be very clear. We are *not* talking about learning in the general, feel-good sense of the word. And, we are certainly not imagining that any senior executive would be happy to hear a statement like, "Hey, boss, the project failed, but let me tell you, I feel like I learned a *ton!*"

Instead, we are referring to a very specific and con-crete form of learning. For our purposes, learning is defined as *improvement in the accuracy of predictions.*

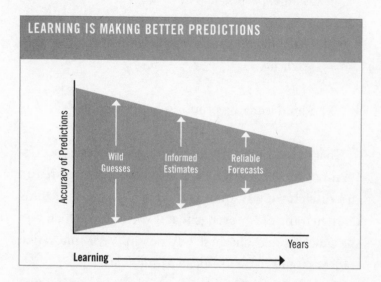

Learning is a process. Every plan for an innovation initiative has some wild guesses in it. Over time, learn-ing will turn those wild guesses into more informed es-timates, and then later turn those informed estimates into reliable forecasts.

Learning should take priority over results because *faster learning leads to better results.* There is a crystal clear logic here. With better predictions, you make bet-ter decisions, and when you make better decisions, you get better results. Learning first, profits second.

Three Fundamental Ideas

1 ▶ Every innovation initiative is properly regarded as an experiment.

2 ▶ Disciplined experimentation yields rapid learning.

3 ▶ Rapid learning promises better results.

That said, faster learning hardly guarantees a successful innovation initiative. Even when experiments are run in a disciplined way, there is still risk. What fast learning does guarantee, however, is that if you fail, you'll do it in the quickest and cheapest way possible. All innovation leaders should strive to "spend a little, learn a lot."

Business people do not, in general, get a lot of practice in running disciplined experiments. Experiments, after all, are the domain of scientists. Nonetheless, everyone learns the basics of experimentation, and does so as early as elementary school. The fundamental steps are familiar.

1 ▶ Plan the experiment to test a hypothesis.

2 ▶ Predict what you *think* is going to happen, documenting how you came up with your predictions as clearly as possible.

3 ▶ Execute the experiment, collecting all relevant data.

4 ▶ Analyze. Specifically, compare what you thought was going to happen to what actually happened. It is through a careful analysis of the differences between predictions and outcomes that you learn.

Practicing just the fundamentals can have an enormous impact. The mistakes that we've observed don't relate to the finer points of rigorous experimentation that scientists take pride in their knowledge of, like confirmation biases and skewed sample sets. Instead, the breakdowns are in the basics. If your company adopts just the fundamentals of disciplined experimentation, you'll be a giant step ahead of your peers.

DO NOT LEAVE LEARNING TO INTUITION

Some companies assert that they have adopted an "experiment-and-learn" mind-set, but in reality they don't bring much discipline to the "learn" part of the equation. In effect, they leave the learning to intuition and judgment.

There are a few, very limited, innovation contexts where this is appropriate. When the nature of the experiment is such that it yields rapid, clear, and one-dimensional feedback, lessons learned are straightforward and intuition is sufficient. Model S initiatives, because they are small, sometimes meet this criteria.

Indeed, much of the logic underlying the Toyota Production System is that it creates an environment in which rapid experimentation with clear feedback is possible. For example, Toyota breaks production steps down into small cells with crisply defined inputs and outputs. This makes it possible for each cell to host an inexpensive experiment that delivers quick-and-clear results. Toyota sees this capability as valuable enough to offset the additional costs of work-in-process inventory that the system imposes.

Even though Toyota creates as ideal an environment as possible for experimentation, the company understands that learning through intuition is nonetheless very difficult. As such, Toyota trains its front-line supervisors in the mechanics of formal experimentation.

Outside of Toyota, researchers have extensively explored the accuracy of intuition in interpreting the results of experiments. Bottom line: Outside of the most ideal conditions, humans are rather unskilled at drawing the right conclusions through intuition alone. In fact, when experiments are lengthy and multidimensional, as Model C initiatives inevitably are, any lessons learned derived from intuition are highly suspect. Delays confound the ability to make accurate conjectures about cause and effect, and countless biases affect judgment.

As such, a formal process for experimentation is indispensable.

YOUR EXISTING PLANNING PROCESS IS NOT AN INNOVATION ASSET

Disciplined experimentation requires, first and foremost, a rigorous planning process. Many managers will react to this statement by thinking, "No problem, we have one!" Unfortunately, the planning process for the Performance Engine is not designed for experimentation, it is designed for administration of ongoing operations.

For some innovation initiatives—Model R—this mismatch doesn't pose too much of a problem. Model R initiatives look very much like ongoing operations. They look similar to past efforts, and they are evaluated based on familiar metrics. As such, only a few minor modifications to typical planning routines are required, especially to address specific areas of uncertainty. By and large, the dominant uncertainty in Model R initiatives is whether or not customers will like the new product. Companies that are well practiced in launching new offerings become quite skilled at analyzing post-launch trends to make as quick a determination as possible whether the new product is on track to success or failure.

Out in Model C terrain, however, the story is much different. The specific attributes of Performance Engine planning processes are wrong in nearly every respect. To give a few examples, a good innovation plan is written on a blank page; Performance Engine plans are based on past precedent. A good innovation plan highlights assumptions; Performance Engine plans highlight facts. A good innovation plan includes a custom scorecard; Performance Engine plans use standard scorecards. A good innovation plan emphasizes trends; Performance Engine plans highlight quarterly and yearly totals. A good innovation plan is readily modified; Performance Engine plans are storehouses for firm expectations. A good innovation plan motivates learning; Performance Engine plans motivate results.

How Performance Engine Planning and Innovation Planning Differ

Performance Engine Plans	Innovation Plans
Based on precedent	Start with a blank page
Emphasize data	Emphasize assumptions
Standard scorecard	Custom scorecard
Highlight quarterly and yearly totals	Highlight trends
Hold firm expectations	Expectations often adjusted
Focused on results	Focused on learning

Recall that the Model C's core strategy for dealing with the Performance Engine is *separation* (as opposed to Model S, which squeezes innovation into the slack in the system, or Model R, which makes innovation look as much like the Performance Engine as possible). We saw, in Part II, how to create a separate and distinct Dedicated Team. Now, we turn our attention to what it takes to create a separate plan, a separate planning process, and a separate planning forum. Performance Engine planning and innovation planning simply do not mix.

In the next three chapters, we will take a closer look at:

1 ▶ *Creating a Structure for Disciplined Experimentation.* We will look at the overall attributes of a

healthy and separate planning track for innovation.

2 ▶ *Breaking Down the Hypothesis.* We will zero in on the most essential attributes of a solid plan for an innovation initiative.

3 ▶ *Seeking the Truth.* We will closely examine the pitfalls that get in the way of drawing accurate lessons learned.

CHAPTER 10

CREATE A STRUCTURE
FOR DISCIPLINED EXPERIMENTATION

As we described in the previous chapter, a separate and parallel planning process for Model C innovation initiatives is a crucial step forward. In this chapter, we focus on the basic process mechanics that are necessary to support disciplined experimentation. There are four essential principles:

1 ▶ Create a separate, stand-alone, custom plan with custom metrics for each initiative.

2 ▶ Discuss results and lessons learned in a separate forum.

3 ▶ Meet frequently.

4 ▶ Expect to make a heavy investment of time and energy.

Let's take a closer look at the logic supporting each of these four principles.

PRINCIPLE #1: EACH INITIATIVE REQUIRES A SEPARATE, STAND-ALONE, CUSTOM PLAN WITH CUSTOM PERFORMANCE METRICS

Performance Engine plans look quite similar from one year to the next. This saves a great deal of time. It allows companies to create standard cost categories, standard performance metrics, and standard templates to fill out during each year's planning cycle. It also allows for the use of information systems that automate some aspects of the planning process.

None of this is possible, however, for Model C innovation initiatives. Plans must be written on a blank page. Just as each Model C initiative requires a custom Dedicated Team, each should be assumed to require a unique plan. That means no shortcuts and no mindless copying of past documents.

The last thing you want to do when assembling the Dedicated Team is default to the same people, same titles and job descriptions, and same hierarchy that you're accustomed to. The rule is the same here. When writing the plan, you start from scratch.

After all, innovation initiatives are very intentional efforts to break away from past practice. Injecting Performance Engine cost categories, performance metrics, or planning templates into innovation plans may save time, but it clouds good thinking and good analysis. It focuses attention on the wrong information and encourages the formation of the wrong kinds of expectations.

No doubt your company strives for efficiency in the planning process as it does elsewhere. But this is one area where it makes sense to very deliberately slow things down. You may have to do some manual tallying, for example, to gather the unique performance data that is relevant to your particular initiative.

PRINCIPLE #2: DISCUSS RESULTS AND LESSONS LEARNED IN A SEPARATE FORUM

Within the Performance Engine, it often makes sense to discuss the results from multiple similar programs or business units in a single meeting. Outcomes can be compared; lessons learned shared. You might even spark a productive dose of internal rivalry.

Throwing a Model C initiative into the mix, however, is just not a good idea. Here are three reasons why:

1 ▶ *The conversations are entirely different.* For example, when Performance Engine initiatives fall behind plan, the conversation is all about how to get back on plan. When innovation initiatives fall behind plan, the conversation should prioritize the possibility that the plan was based on faulty assumptions.

2 ▶ *The standards of performance are different.* Innovation initiatives often should be assessed based on distinct performance metrics; or, even if the metric is the same, the standard should be different. We have seen several instances of companies drawing the wrong conclusions about "how things are going" for the innovation initiative because the results were discussed in a forum in which it was instinctive to apply the same performance criteria to everything.

3 ▶ *Small numbers are too easily ignored.* The numbers from the innovation initiative may be so

small relative to the other operations being discussed that they seem like mere round-off errors. Little innovation initiatives get little attention in meetings about big businesses.

Having said this, we would clearly be going too far if we suggested that planning for innovation initiatives could be completely isolated from the Performance Engine. We discussed one crucial area of overlap in Part II—resource planning for the Shared Staff. Capital budgeting is another area where Performance Engine plans and innovation plans intersect. Thus, it is only in the discussion of results and lessons learned that we strongly advocate for isolating the conversation in a separate forum.

PRINCIPLE #3: MEET FREQUENTLY

If learning is good, then quick learning is even better, especially if there are millions of dollars at risk. The normal interval for in-depth reviews of Performance Engine plans is once per year. This isn't nearly frequent enough for innovation initiatives.

The innovation planning forum should meet at least as often as there might be new data that challenges or confirms the assumptions in the plan. This could be quarterly, or even monthly. The rate at which you learn is directly limited by the frequency at which you review your assumptions, and, potentially, revise your plan.

PRINCIPLE #4: MAKE A HEAVY INVESTMENT OF TIME AND ENERGY

Business people tend not to want to spend a great deal of time on plans for innovation initiatives. The feeling seems to be that since the uncertainties are high the plans can't be worth much. Better to identify a general direction of travel and then improvise.

This line of thinking is fallacious. The value of the predictions in a plan for an innovation initiative does not lie in their accuracy. The predictions are valuable because they can later serve as starting points for analysis. If the predictions turn out to be wrong, you know you have to alter the underlying hypothesis. This is how you learn.

Another reason that innovation plans receive inadequate attention is that when senior executives allocate their attention across numerous plans throughout a company, the natural tendency is to allocate time in proportion to the size of the budget. Since innovation initiatives start out tiny, they may get little attention at all. A better guideline would be to allocate time based on potential bottom-line impact or potential contribution to long-term growth. Doing so would shine a much brighter spotlight on innovation.

Realistically, innovation plans require substantially *more* time and energy than Performance Engine plans. That's because when you draw up a plan for the Performance Engine, you can simply make a few modifications from the prior year's plan—a few percentage points of growth here, a cost-cutting initiative there. Innovation initiatives, by contrast, have no history. They are brand new, and predictions must be made from scratch. It just takes longer.

More time is also required when evaluating results. In the Performance Engine, there are well-known metrics and well-understood standards of performance. Figuring out whether it was a good quarter or a bad quarter is just a matter of comparing results to these benchmarks. The picture is quite a bit more complicated for an innovation initiative. The question is whether the initiative is on a *trajectory* to success. The uncertainties are high, the data incomplete, and the performance metrics unfamiliar. Judging how things are going simply takes longer.

The four principles in this chapter—create a separate plan, create a separate forum, meet frequently, and invest substantial time and energy—are straightforward. What is often harder, however, is sustaining the commitment to disciplined experimentation that these principles imply.

And, there is more to disciplined experimentation than just the mechanics described here. In the remaining two chapters, we examine how to establish a clear and testable hypothesis of record and how best to shape conversations about results.

CHAPTER 11

BREAK DOWN THE HYPOTHESIS

N ot long ago, while working with a group of innovation teams, we asked each to describe the hypothesis that was guiding their efforts. One team responded, "Our hypothesis is that this initiative is going to generate enormous profits." They then went on to estimate the profits that were possible.

There is nothing wrong, of course, with shooting for bottom-line success. However, a hypothesis that focuses attention only on the bottom line is unlikely to lead to quick learning. It does not help a team "spend a little, learn a lot." By the time you know for sure whether you are going to get the bottom-line results you anticipate, you have already spent an enormous sum.

Therefore, it is crucial to break down the hypothesis

into smaller, discrete assumptions that can be tested along the road to success. By doing so, you create the opportunity for regular confirmations that you are on track. These periodic wins keep a team motivated. Equally important, you create an early warning system that alerts you to the need to change directions (or possibly abandon the initiative) before a disappointing failure becomes an unbearably expensive failure.

In this chapter, after cautioning against overreliance on spreadsheets, we will show a method for breaking down a hypothesis, which involves documenting specific cause-and-effect conjectures, creating a custom scorecard, and predicting outcomes.

BE AWARE OF THE LIMITATIONS OF SPREADSHEETS

Most companies, before launching a significant innovation initiative, will require the production of a business case analysis that shows that the investment can yield an acceptable return on investment. Usually, these analyses are assembled using spreadsheet programs. While spreadsheets are powerful machines for business analysis, they are generally inadequate to support team learning as an innovation initiative proceeds. They suffer from at least three shortfalls:

1 ▶ *Spreadsheets hide assumptions.* When you open a spreadsheet, what you see are numbers. If you want to try to understand how those numbers were calculated, you have to go through a relatively painful process of reverse engineering the spreadsheet by studying dozens of algebraic equations. If spreadsheet builders are honest with themselves, they will admit that untangling the logic of *even their own spreadsheets* can be a frustrating and lengthy process, once some time has passed since they created the spreadsheet.

2 ▶ *Spreadsheets focus attention in the wrong place—on the numbers themselves.* A focus on the numbers is suitable for the Performance Engine, wherein judging performance is mostly a matter of comparing measured outcomes to well-known and well-understood performance standards. For innovation initiatives, however, judging performance is much more subjective. There simply are no well-known, well-understood performance standards.

3 ▶ *Spreadsheets create an illusion of precision.* With so many big tables of figures, often calculated to several decimal points, it is easy to imagine that the numbers are far more accurate than they

really are. This illusion can take a conversation about the performance of an innovation initiative exactly where it should not go—into the nuances of how the numbers in the spreadsheet were calculated. Instead, conversations should focus on fundamental assumptions, with recognition that the uncertainties are large.

We are not arguing against the use of spreadsheets. Instead, we are suggesting that their use should be coupled with other tools that are more aligned with the realities of innovation and more conducive to conversations focused on learning.

WHAT ARE WE SPENDING MONEY ON? AND, WHY?

The conversations that lead most quickly to learning are those that are focused on the fundamental assumptions that guide an innovation initiative. Though the technique is not foolproof, most of these assumptions can be identified by asking just two common sense questions:

1 ▶ What are we spending money on?

2 ▶ Why?

The first question is best addressed by dividing the budget into a handful (say, five or so) of categories. Note that employees and their time are often the bulk of an innovation initiative's expenditures, especially early on. Thus, the categories should include staff time.

Let's take a look at a hypothetical example that we will continue to expand over the next few pages.

> Imagine that you are building a new Internet-based business that provides consumers with expert advice on new products and services. Imagine, for simplicity, that advertising is the only revenue source for this initiative.
>
> Such an initiative might include five major budget categories—market research, content, marketing, information technology, and sales.

The answer to the second question—*Why?*—must be addressed separately for each budget category. What are the specific outcomes that you expect to achieve as a result of the dollars spent? It may be easiest, at first, to simply create a list of desired outcomes, both operational and financial.

> Let's start with just one budget category, marketing. The list of desired outcomes includes: 1) increased revenues, 2) increased users on

our website, 3) increased pages viewed, and
4) increased advertisements sold.

The heart of any innovation hypothesis, however, is more than just a list of desired outcomes. Instead, it is a set of statements that describe cause and effect. It is a collection of *if–then* conjectures that connect actions (most often, what you are spending money on) to outcomes.

A simple but extremely effective technique for focusing conversations on cause-and-effect conjectures is to create diagrams that present the relationships between actions and outcomes in a simple visual language. Unidirectional arrows intuitively convey cause and effect.

If we spend on marketing, *then* the number of users on our website will rise.

Marketing Spending ⟶ Website Users

Most often, innovation hypotheses involve chains of causality, not single cause-and-effect connections. For any near-term outcome, there may be one or more subsequent outcomes, each dependent on prior outcomes, like a column of dominoes toppling, one after the other.

> If we increase the number of users on our website, then the number of pages viewed will go up. If the number of pages viewed rises, we will have the opportunity to sell more ads. If we sell more ads, revenues will rise.

Marketing Spending → Website Users → Page Views → Ads Sold → Revenues

A separate causal chain should be created for each major spending category. Inevitably, some outcomes, particularly financial outcomes like revenues, will show up on multiple causal chains. The next step, therefore, is to create a single diagram that connects the chains to each other. Each outcome should appear just once on the combined diagram.

> If we spend to create compelling content, our customers will view more pages on each visit to our website. This, in turn, will increase total pages viewed, ads sold, and revenues. (This process could then be continued for the remaining three spending categories.)

Content Spending → Pages Viewed per Visit

Marketing Spending → Website Users → Page Views → Ads Sold → Revenues

Note that actions always lie at the root of the chains: Action, then a near-term outcome, then subsequent outcomes.

Next, it is worthwhile to consider actions *other than spending* that will have a significant impact on outcomes. The most common example is pricing decisions. It is also worthwhile to consider adding actions that could be taken *outside of your company,* particularly actions taken by direct competitors.

> The price that the we charge for advertisements will have an impact on both the number of advertisements sold and revenues. Also, marketing spending by a direct rival will also have an impact on the number of users we attract.

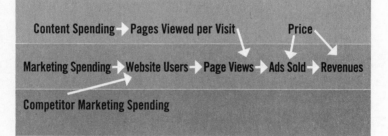

For many initiatives, the number of actions and outcomes that *could* be placed on the diagram is enormous. We worked with one team that literally filled a wall. As such, it is important to remember that these diagrams are meant to support good *conversations* about assumptions. Everyone involved in the conversation must be able to quickly review and understand the map every time there is a meeting to review progress. A diagram that does not fit on one printed page, with no more than about twenty-five cause-and-effect connections, is just too big for this purpose.

Even with a diagram that fits on one page, there is a risk that too much complexity will undermine productive learning conversations. To further simplify, identify the *critical unknowns* on the map. These are the causal connections that are both uncertain and consequential. (If you have taken a big guess and you are sunk if the guess is wrong, that's a critical unknown.) It is good practice to highlight the critical unknowns on the cause-and-effect map. Focus conversations here first. And, if there is a way to test these assumptions quickly and easily, make it a priority to do so.

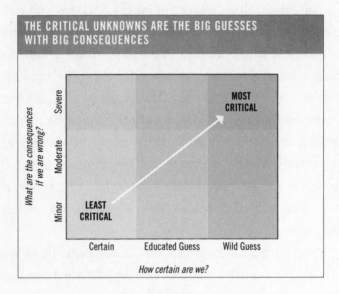

THE CRITICAL UNKNOWNS ARE THE BIG GUESSES WITH BIG CONSEQUENCES

BUILD A CUSTOM SCORECARD

Just by producing the causal map you are well on your way to completing the next crucial step, creating a custom scorecard. In the absence of one, it becomes all too easy to fall back on Performance Engine metrics and standards, which cannot be assumed to be relevant for Model C initiatives.

All of the outcomes on the causal map are potential metrics. For those that are not directly measurable, consider whether it is worthwhile to identify a *proxy*—something measurable that is likely to be closely correlated to the outcome of interest.

The metrics that are closest to the root of each chain are *leading indicators*—the results that will give the first alerts if the initiative has gone awry, or if one of the cause-and-effect conjectures has proven false. Watch the leading indicators and you will spend a little, and learn a lot.

Because innovation initiatives are intentional departures from past precedent, your company may have no data gathering or data processing infrastructure in place to automate the process of collecting the performance data you need. Populating your scorecard with actual numbers, therefore, may require substantial additional effort. If resources are constrained, you'll naturally want to focus first on gathering the data that can validate or invalidate your most critical unknowns.

GO AHEAD, PUT A STAKE IN THE GROUND

Recall that the most crucial step in running a disciplined experiment is assessing lessons learned by comparing what you thought was going to happen to what actually happened—that is, by comparing predictions to outcomes. Sometimes, the notion of trying to predict makes people break out in hives. *How can we predict? There is so much uncertainty!* However, what is required is not a highly accurate prediction, just one that is consistent with the cause-and-effect hypothesis. Remember, the value of the prediction is not in its accuracy, it is in its subsequent use as a benchmark for learning and analysis.

When reviewing results, the primary question of interest is: *Are we on a trajectory to success?* Answering this question does not require comparing predictions to outcomes to the third decimal place. In fact, rather than comparing number to number, it is most sensible to compare trend to trend. Aggregate totals for a quarter or a year mean little compared to week-to-week or month-to-month trends. When your initiative produces a trend that is different from the predicted trend, you may have evidence that one of your underlying assumptions, usually a conjecture about cause and effect, might be false.

Trends are more relevant than numbers because innovation initiatives are very dynamic. This is in contrast to the Performance Engine, where each period is mostly similar to the one that preceded it. The difference is analogous to that between watching the dials in the cockpit of an airplane during takeoff and doing so while flying at a steady course, speed, and altitude. In the first case, all the dials are in motion; in the second, they are barely moving at all.

One way to ensure that you stay in the right mind-set is to graph both your budgets and your predictions as trends over time. (This is, again, intended as a supplement to, not a replacement for, the use of spreadsheets.) To produce a trend graph for the budget, take your best guess at the amount you anticipate spending at some point in the future (i.e., by the end of the second year, we expect to employ one hundred software developers), and sketch a trajectory for getting from where you are today to that future benchmark.

A similar process for predictions works well. You might, for example, make a ballpark guess at the number of customers you expect to be serving one year from now, and then sketch, roughly, what you expect the trajectory to that target will be. Will the trajectory be linear, with the same number of customers gained each quarter? Or, will it be exponential, with most of the gain coming in the fourth quarter? Will there be any delays between actions and outcomes?

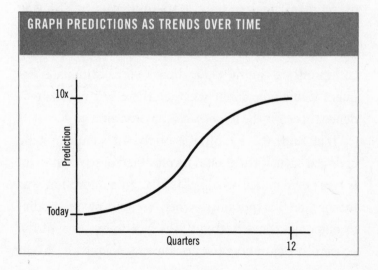

GRAPH PREDICTIONS AS TRENDS OVER TIME

Because innovation initiatives are by nature worse-before-better gambles (you have to invest short-term to win long-term), many innovation metrics follow a worse-before-better trajectory. It is particularly important to talk these through. How deep will the trough be? How long will it take to get through it? For example, imagine that you are hiring a software team. Because the task of training new hires will distract the more seasoned veterans from coding, you might anticipate that hiring will make the team's total productivity go down before it goes up.

Taken together, cause-and-effect diagrams, budget trends, and outcome trends represent a formal hypothesis for testing. Everyone directly involved with an innovation initiative should be familiar with the hypothesis of record, particularly the critical unknowns. Indeed, why not post the cause-and-effect diagrams, budget trends, and outcome trends in a public place? Doing so will help communicate the hypothesis, as well as stimulate frequent discussion about whether there is any new evidence that calls the hypothesis into question.

That said, the hypothesis of record should not be changed casually. It should be modified only when there is clear evidence that suggests that an assumption was inaccurate. Furthermore, when comparing prediction to outcome, trend to trend, it is best to be wary of the possibility of jumping to a conclusion too quickly. When you do not get the trend that you predicted, this does not automatically mean that there is no cause-and-effect relationship. There are actually four possibilities:

1 ▸ The cause-and-effect relationship does not exist.

2 ▸ We have not yet spent enough money to get the predicted impact.

3 ▸ We have not waited long enough for the predicted impact.

4 ▸ There are additional variables that we have not considered that are affecting the desired outcomes.

When you conclude that the cause-and-effect relationship does not exist or is too weak to be relevant, then it is time to make a formal change in direction and a formal update to the cause-and-effect map.

To many, cause-and-effect diagrams and trend graphs might seem very loose, too inaccurate to be of much value. We disagree. They are accurate enough, given the uncertainty that confronts Model C innovation initiatives. They focus conversations where they belong, on cause-and-effect assumptions and on early indications of success or failure.

CHAPTER 12

SEEK THE TRUTH

E ven if you establish a robust separate planning track
for innovation initiatives and communicate a hypothesis of record with dazzling clarity, there is still
one major pitfall that stands in the way of rapid learning. It is a dangerous one, perhaps even the biggest bar-
rier to innovation within established organizations. It
arises in a single meeting—when the innovation leader
sits down with the boss to have a conversation about
whether they have been doing a good job or a poor job.
In this chapter, we will: 1) show why innovation leaders
should be evaluated differently from Performance Engine leaders, 2) outline a specific approach for evaluating
innovation leaders, and 3) discuss how to help innovation leaders avoid bias in judging results.

PERFORMANCE EVALUATION IN THE PERFORMANCE ENGINE

In most companies, there is one dominant question that shapes whether a manager gets a good review or a poor one. Did they, or did they not, hit their numbers? Some companies are maniacal about enforcing this discipline. It's results, results, results. Deliver the goods and you get promoted. Fail to deliver the goods and you may be forgiven . . . but probably not more than once.

Such discipline generally works well in the Performance Engine, but it is important to understand why. First, recognize that any effort to evaluate performance is based on a comparison between an outcome and a prediction. The outcome comes from the actions of managers; the prediction comes from a theory, model, or hypothesis, about how the business will perform.

The Performance Engine is guided by a very simple theory: This period will look a lot like last period. That makes predicting straightforward, and it makes predictions accurate more often than not. If results fall short of predictions, then putting pressure on managers to get back on target is a reasonable response—just so long as ongoing operations are reliably predictable.

IT IS NOT SO EASY
FOR INNOVATION INITIATIVES

Plans for innovation initiatives should *not* be presumed accurate. There is no history. There is no reasonable expectation that this period will look a lot like last period. And, as we saw in the previous chapter, there is ample guesswork in every Model C innovation hypothesis.

Therefore, the right action when outcomes fall short is *not* to immediately jump to the conclusion that managers are underperforming and pressure them to get back on track. Instead, the right action is to explore the possibility that the hypothesis might be wrong.

Recall that we defined learning as improvement in the accuracy of predictions. Note that if you assume that your predictions are right . . . if you are unwilling to modify your predictions as you gain more information . . . if all you know how to do is demand that managers get back on track . . . then your predictions can't possibly get better. You can't possibly, over time, convert wild guesses into informed estimates into reliable predictions. You can't possibly spend a little, and learn a lot. You can't possibly learn, period.

As devastating as that is, the consequences of presuming that predictions are accurate and holding innovation leaders accountable to plan run even deeper:

1 ▶ *Innovation leaders will spend no time questioning the validity of their assumptions.* If they fall behind plan, rather than trying to learn and adjust, they will simply redouble their efforts to somehow get back on track, working nights and weekends, and asking everyone involved to do the same. If there is a fatally flawed assumption in the plan, of course, late hours won't help.

2 ▶ *Innovation leaders will never be willing to pull the plug on a failing initiative.* As they will see it, the only option is to keep trying and hope for a miraculous turnaround.

3 ▶ *Innovation leaders will avoid engaging in open learning conversations with their superiors.* They will understand, all too well, that any admission that the plan might be wrong is an admission of defeat.

4 ▶ *Innovation leaders will set low aspirations.* Instead of aiming high and focusing on clarity of assumptions when proposing an innovation plan, they will engage in game playing. They will try to find the outcomes that are just barely high enough to get the plan approved.

Therefore, predictions in the plan must be assumed wrong. Indeed, everyone involved must be comfortable with the reality that innovation leaders have a great deal in common with soothsayers with a crystal ball. Both are in the business of making predictions that are probably wrong.

That said, accepting that the predictions are probably wrong is hard to do. It is anathema to what happens in the Performance Engine, wherein the predictions in the plan are practically sacred. They represent your solemn promise. It's what you, as a manager, agree to deliver.

Furthermore, accepting that predictions are probably wrong implies routinely engaging in conversations about the assumptions, theories, and models that the predictions are based upon. These are unfamiliar waters for executives acculturated in the Performance Engine, where facts and data, not assumptions and theories, are the constant focus. These stark differences further underline the importance of creating a separate forum for evaluating innovation initiatives and their leaders.

INNOVATION LEADERS MUST BE EVALUATED DIFFERENTLY, BUT WITH NO LESS DISCIPLINE

We've sometimes said that companies ought to have a blue form for individual performance evaluations of

Performance Engine leaders and a yellow form for innovation leaders. Indeed, there is very little relationship between the two.

In making this statement, we've experienced a backlash. Performance Engine leaders who sweat it out each day trying to ensure that they are on time, on budget, and on spec will instinctively resent the possibility that someone else might be evaluated on standards that seem lax by comparison. Senior executives, for their part, might recoil at the notion of treating anyone differently for fear that doing so will undermine the culture of accountability that many associate so strongly with consistent results.

The alternative to accountability to plan, however, is not chaos. It is a different form of accountability, one that is just as demanding and just as rigorous. Instead of being held accountable for delivering the results in the plan, innovation leaders ought to be held accountable for learning. They ought to be held accountable for running a disciplined experiment.

This does make performance appraisal more subjective, because the focus of evaluation shifts from an *outcome* to a *process*. As such, closer and more frequent observation of innovation leaders is necessary. The specific evaluation points, however, are straightforward:

1 ▶ *Is the innovation leader investing sufficient time and energy in planning and analyzing results?*

Learning should be grounded in careful analysis of the disparities between predictions and outcomes. Doing this well takes time and energy. Beware the innovation leader who wants to discard the plan because it is "full of wild guesses anyway."

2 ▶ *Is there a clear hypothesis of record?* Is it easy to understand? Is everyone on the team able to articulate it in much the same way?

3 ▶ *Are the critical unknowns clear and well understood?* Which assumptions are shakiest? Of those, which are most consequential? Is everyone on the team highly aware of the critical unknowns?

4 ▶ *How do changes in the plan come about?* There should not be a significant change in plan without data that supports a clear lesson learned. Innovation leaders should not make significant changes just because "it feels like the right thing to do."

5 ▶ *Is the innovation leader trying to learn quickly and cheaply?* Are the assumptions being checked frequently—as often as there might be new data

that might call them into question? Is every possible avenue to testing the critical unknowns quickly and cheaply being pursued?

6 ▶ *Is the innovation leader willing to face the facts, even when they are unpleasant?* The more time, energy, heart, and soul an innovation leader pours into an innovation initiative, the harder it becomes to acknowledge when the initiative is on a track to disappointment. The best innovation leaders are always humble enough to explicitly consider the possibility.

7 ▶ *Are predictions improving?* There is no more direct evidence of learning than improvement in predictions. Every innovation initiative's custom scorecard can include some indication of accuracy of predictions.

These evaluation points are tough and demanding. No Performance Engine leader who closely examines them will conclude that innovation leaders have it easy. The best way to squelch tensions over fairness of individual performance appraisals is to acknowledge very clearly that innovation leaders are measured by a different yardstick . . . but one that is every bit as difficult and demanding as any other.

CREATE AN ATMOSPHERE
OF SCIENTIFIC DETACHMENT

Because innovation leaders are often too close to the problem to analyze results in a dispassionate matter, many will benefit from a partner who acts as a foil ... someone well versed in the analytic rigor that goes with disciplined experimentation, and someone who is willing to ask the tough questions from a point of emotional detachment. An executive with experience in the venture capital investing community may be able to play this role well, as might a seasoned scientist from a company's R&D group.

This person should actively participate in every review of how the innovation initiative is doing. He or she should try, as best possible, to create an environment of open inquiry and discussion—one that focuses on learning and assumption testing, and one that is free of bias.

It is important to recognize that innovation leaders are in a position in which they must *sell* the potential of their initiatives practically every day—to customers, to executive sponsors, and to their staffs. That said, reviews of how the initiative is doing should be "sales-free zones." The only questions that matter are: "What new results do we have?" and "Do these results call any of our assumptions into question?"

During these discussions, the detached foil can look for several specific biases and try to eliminate them from the conversation. He or she should ask: Are we drawing conclusions that are politically convenient? Are we jumping to the conclusion that a particular outcome was caused by something obvious—a recent action or a sizable spending choice? Are we defaulting to explanations that are familiar in our core business, but may not apply to this initiative? Are we biased to conclusions that shift the blame away from the actions of our core team?

Most critically, he or she must ensure that everyone is acting as though the predictions are probably wrong, not probably right. The goal is not to deliver on plan. It is to learn, and learn fast.

KEY LESSONS LEARNED

To conclude, we list *Beyond the Idea*'s most fundamental principles for innovation:

1 ▶ Companies must shift time and energy from *this side* to the *other side* of innovation—from a focus on ideas to a focus on execution.

2 ▶ Organizations are not built for innovation, they are built for ongoing operations . . . and there are fundamental incompatibilities between the two.

3 ▶ There are three powerful models for overcoming these incompatibilities and allowing innovation and ongoing operations to simultaneously thrive. All three models can coexist in a single company, but it is crucial to match each initiative to the proper model.

    a. Model S, for *Small* initiatives, attempts to squeeze innovation into small slivers of slack time. It can deliver a very large number of very small initiatives.

b. Model R, for *Repeatable* initiatives, attempts to make innovation as repeatable and predictable as possible. It can deliver an ongoing series of similar initiatives, regardless of their size.

c. Model C, for *Custom* initiatives, is for all initiatives that are beyond the limitations of either Model S or Model R.

4 ▶ Model C has two components: a Special Team and a Special Plan. Each Model C initiative requires its own custom-designed Special Team and Special Plan.

5 ▶ The Special Team is a partnership between two groups of people—a Dedicated Team and a Shared Staff. The Dedicated Team is dedicated full-time or very nearly full-time to just one Model C initiative. The Shared Staff has simultaneous responsibilities for both the innovation initiative and ongoing operations.

6 ▶ The Shared Staff may only take on familiar tasks or tasks that it can learn quickly and readily in-

corporate into day-to-day operations. Furthermore, the Shared Staff can only take on tasks that fit into existing roles, responsibilities, and workflows. The Dedicated Team must take on all other innovation tasks.

7 ▶ Build the Dedicated Team as though you are building a new organization from the ground up, custom designed for the task at hand. This typically involves hiring outsiders, creating new roles, shaping a new hierarchy, and even creating a distinct culture.

8 ▶ The partnership between the Dedicated Team and the Shared Staff is never an easy one. Keeping it healthy requires a positive and collaborative innovation leader, an engaged senior leadership team, and a Shared Staff that is adequately resourced to do both of its jobs.

9 ▶ A Model C initiative requires a Special Plan, one that is written for disciplined experimentation and rapid learning.

10 ▶ Planning systems for established organizations are designed for administration of ongoing operations, not for disciplined experimentation.

Therefore, Model C initiatives need both a separate plan and a separate forum for discussing results.

11 ▶ At the heart of the Special Plan is a clear hypothesis of record, one that lays out the conjectures about cause and effect that connect planned actions with hoped-for results.

12 ▶ Innovation leaders must be evaluated based on criteria that are demanding but distinct from the yardsticks used to assess leaders of ongoing operations. Innovation leaders must be evaluated based primarily on how well they run a disciplined experiment.

APPENDICES

RELATED TOPICS

APPENDIX 1. **STRATEGY**

No Performance Engine lasts forever. That's why innovation is so critical to the long-term vitality of any organizations. As such, over the long run, strategy and innovation are tightly coupled.

We have focused on the execution challenge in *Beyond the Idea*. In this appendix, however, we offer a framework that brings together both the front end and the back end of the innovation challenge: both strategy and execution, both thinking and doing.

At the core of that framework is an observation that everything that a company thinks and does can be put into one of the three boxes. Box 1 is: Manage the Present. Box 2 is: Selectively Forget the Past. Box 3 is: Create the Future.

Most companies expend almost all of their energies

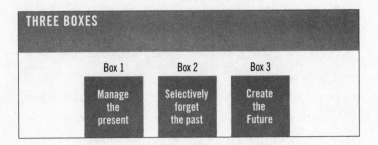

in Box 1. Of course, sustaining excellence in the Performance Engine is critically important. Box 1, however, does not give you transformation. It does not give companies the adaptability that is necessary to endure through mammoth changes in the business environment, such as globalization, technological advance, regulatory change, or demographic shifts. To get there, you need Box 2 and Box 3.

Perhaps the most challenging of the three boxes is Box 2. The word *selectively* in Box 2 is crucial. It's not *abandon* the past, it is *selectively forget* the past. The Performance Engine will continue to operate on its current logic. It must continue to strive for the best possible performance.

That said, the first step in generating Box 3 ideas for breakthrough innovation is freeing one's thinking from constraints. In other words, Box 2 is a prerequisite for Box 3. Box 2 requires challenging the enduring assumptions of the Performance Engine. At the most basic level:

Who are your customers? What do they value? How do you deliver that value?

Box 2 also demands willingness to break your company's rules or your industry's rules. Instead of benchmarking what your competition is doing, you imagine what *none* of your competitors are doing. Instead of focusing only on the demands of your biggest customers, you pay heed to leading-edge customers, the ones who may define your industry's future. Instead of containing your thinking within each of your corporation's business units, you ask what is possible if the skills and assets within these units were combined in new ways for new purposes. Instead of asking what's possible with current skills and assets, you imagine what your company could build in the long run. Instead of only imagining what is possible this year, you consider what's possible in five years or ten.

If you completely break free of constraints, the world is wide open in Box 3. Such freedom can be both liberating and overwhelming. Progress can be accelerated by shaping thinking with a long-term, ambitious, aspirational goal—a strategic intent. The most effective statements of strategic intent combine a clear direction of travel with a challenge that seems almost impossible to achieve. Some good examples include Google's intent to "organize the world's information," or, many decades back, Honda's desire to put "six Hondas in a two-car garage" (by adding, say, a lawn mower, a motorcycle, a snowmobile, and a leaf blower).

Once you commit to a Box 3 idea, then comes the execution phase, the core focus in *Beyond the Idea*. Box 3 ideas always require Model C execution. (Box 1 ideas might require Model S, R, or C, depending on the nature of the initiative and the capabilities of the organization. See chapters 2, 3, and 4. As Box 2 is about *forgetting*, there are no Box 2 ideas. Ideas are either Box 1 or Box 3.)

As a Model C initiative proceeds, Box 2, selective forgetting, remains crucial. Where failure to challenge strategic orthodoxies is the front-end Box 2 problem, failure to challenge organizational norms and planning norms is the execution phase Box 2 problem. In fact, we have been talking about selectively forgetting throughout this book.

Consider, in particular, the discussion in chapter 7, forming the Dedicated Team. The primary error here is to create a Little Performance Engine rather than a Dedicated Team. This happens when companies fail to forget, instead defaulting to existing organizational routines. They use the same people, insist on the same titles and job descriptions, make no effort to shift the hierarchy, sustain the same culture, and stick with the existing policies in crucial functions like human resources. Creating a plan for a Model C initiative also requires selective forgetting, including the rhythm of reviews, the metrics used to assess progress, and the criteria by which the innovation leader is evaluated.

Box 3 thinking also remains important in the execution phase of a Model C initiative. Both the special kind of team and the special kind of plan are created from the ground up, from a blank page. This can seem daunting, just like coming up with Box 3 ideas. Identifying analogies can help, but it is essential to seek analogies from *outside* your company. If you are a manufacturing company that is expanding into value-added software, for example, the right place to look for inspiration for shaping the Special Team and the Special Plan is the software industry, not your own company.

APPENDIX 2. **CHANGE**

Innovation and change are similar challenges. They both involve encouraging employees to move in new directions. As a result, innovation initiatives and change initiatives often end up mixed together on the strategic agenda. This can be confusing, and we recommend separating the two.

Innovation is about experimentation. Innovation initiatives are launched with a full understanding that the outcome is uncertain. Failure *is* an option. The goal is to learn quickly, so that if failure comes, it comes fast and cheap.

Because of innovation's experimental nature, it is crucial to take steps to *avoid any impact on the Performance Engine*. We have kept this objective at the top of our minds while writing this book. It is, for example, why we advise such caution in assigning tasks to the Shared Staff (see chapter 6). The innovation mantra is: "Try it and see if it works ... while doing no harm to our day-to-day business."

Change initiatives are quite the opposite. Companies undertake change initiatives when the destination is clear and clearly desirable. Failure is *not* an option. Change is *not*, at its foundation, about experimentation. Further, while the innovation model we've outlined in *Beyond the Idea avoids* any impact on the Performance Engine, a change initiative *strives for* impact on the Performance Engine. That's the entire point, in fact. Instead of creating a Dedicated Team that operates differently from the rest of the company, you ask the *entire company* to operate differently. The change mantra is not, "Try it and see if it works," it is: "Just do it."

That said, innovation and change are often interrelated. Consider these possibilities:

1 ▶ Sometimes innovation leads to change. For example, a company might launch a new business to serve existing customers. That's an innovation initiative. Then, once the new business is proven, it might be very clear that a redesigned and combined sales process for both businesses would be more efficient. That's a change initiative.

2 ▶ A change effort can sometimes include smaller innovation efforts. For example, a change effort to make a company more customer focused and less product focused might include an experimental launch of a new customer support service.

3 ▶ Change can sometimes lead to innovation. For example, a company could redesign its IT systems to be more Internet friendly. That's a change initiative that might affect everyone in the company. Once the new systems are in place, many innovation initiatives might become newly possible.

Even though innovation and change are closely related and one often leads to the other, it's quite helpful to differentiate your company's innovation agenda from its change agenda. The prescriptions in *Beyond the Idea* apply only to innovation.

APPENDIX 3.
THE CHIEF INNOVATION OFFICER

Although the title of Chief Innovation Officer is popping up in more and more corporations, the job descriptions that are attached to the title vary widely. Most often, however, the job focuses on the front end—*this side* of innovation. We'd like to see much of that energy shifted to the execution phase, the *other side* of innovation. We suggest attention to the following tasks:

1 ▶ Create separate pipelines and separate management routines for Model S, Model R, and Model C initiatives. (See chapters 1–4.)

2 ▶ Advocate for resources for Model C initiatives, with an eye toward *all* of the resources that will be necessary to execute. Be sure not to overlook

the necessary time and energy of the Shared Staff. (See chapters 6, 8.)

3 ▶ Be directly involved in shaping the organizational design of Dedicated Teams for Model C initiatives, considering analogies from outside industries where appropriate. (See chapter 7.)

4 ▶ Take the lead in adjudicating conflicts between Model C initiatives and the Performance Engine. Anticipate that this will require more direct interaction at lower levels in the organization than is typical for senior executives, and that it will take substantial time and energy. (See chapter 8.)

5 ▶ Create a distinct and separate process for evaluating the progress of innovation initiatives. (See chapter 10.)

6 ▶ Ensure that each innovation initiative has a clear hypothesis of record that is stated in the form of conjectures about cause and effect. (See chapter 11.)

7 ▶ Be present in every meeting in which the progress of innovation initiatives are formally assessed. Aim to create an environment that is

nondefensive, analytical, and detached. (See chapters 10, 12.)

8 ▶ Evaluate the personal performance of innovation leaders by assessing whether or not they are running disciplined experiments. (See chapter 12.)

These are all tasks that are worthy of a senior executive's scarce time and energy. As many of these tasks are time-consuming, creating a position for an executive dedicated to these tasks, whether a chief innovation officer or an executive with a different title, is an excellent idea.

Some companies create internal boards of directors for Model C initiatives. This alternative can work, but such boards sometimes suffer from the problem that when several people are collectively accountable, nobody feels accountable. To avoid this problem, assign each of the tasks above to specific board members.

ACKNOWLEDGMENTS

In past books, we have gone to great lengths to acknowledge every contributor. Here, we'd like to do something different. We'd like to acknowledge, collectively, our clients.

This book, more so than any past effort, is a product of our interactions with people who are actively applying our ideas to "live" innovation efforts. Our clients have challenged us, pushed us to work harder, and urged us to achieve ever higher levels of clarity and practicality.

We are deeply in their debt.

INDEX